WITHDRAWN

DATE DUE

APR 1 7 2006			
MAY 1 7 2007			

D0620070

THE LIFE AND ADVENTURES
OF
HENRY BIBB
AN AMERICAN SLAVE

Henry Bibb

With a new introduction by
Charles J. Heglar

The University of Wisconsin Press

The University of Wisconsin Press
2537 Daniels Street
Madison, Wisconsin 53718

3 Henrietta Street
London WC2E 8LU, England

Printed in the United States of America

Library of Congress Cataloging-in-Publication Data

Bibb, Henry, b. 1815.
   [Narrative of the life and adventures of Henry Bibb]
   The life and adventures of Henry Bibb : an American slave /
Henry Bibb; with a new introduction by Charles J. Heglar.
   pp.   cm.
   Originally published: Narrative of the life and adventures of
Henry Bibb. New York : H. Bibb, 1849.
   Includes bibliographical references.
   ISBN 0-299-16890-5 (cloth: alk. paper)
   ISBN 0-299-16894-8 (pbk.: alk. paper)
   1. Bibb, Henry, b. 1815.   2. Slaves—United States—Biography.
3. Slaves—Kentucky—Social conditions—19th century.   4. Slav-
ery—Kentucky—History—19th century.
I. Heglar, Charles J.   II. Title.
E444 .B58   2001
976.9′00496—dc21   00-042307

INTRODUCTION

I

The year 1999 marked one hundred and fifty years since the initial publication of Henry Bibb's *Narrative of the Life and Adventures of Henry Bibb, An American Slave; Written by Himself.* While most general discussions of antebellum slave narratives mention Bibb as one of the more interesting writers in the genre, his *Life and Adventures* has not been readily available to general or academic readers for some years. This is especially unfortunate considering the current critical importance of Frederick Douglass's *Narrative of the Life of Frederick Douglass, An American Slave; Written by Himself* (1845) and Harriet Jacobs' *Incidents in the Life of a Slave Girl; Written by Herself* (1861) in the study of slave narratives and, consequently, in the study of African American literature. Bibb's *Life and Adventures* adds new and important dimensions to the examination of the pre–Civil War slave narrative in the areas of slave marriage and family and in the area of plotting and narrative structure.

Since the term *slave narrative* covers many kinds of texts within a heterogeneous genre, it is important to specify the characteristics of the sub-genre in which Bibb, Douglass, and Jacobs wrote. Marion Wilson Starling's comprehensive study, *The Slave Narrative: Its Place in American History* (1981), offers a good overview of the perimeters of the genre; Starling finds that of the slave narratives published between the late seventeenth and the mid-twentieth centuries, six thousand are extant. In addition to this long period of production, Starling notes a range of authorship: some narratives were so heavily and obviously edited that they would be considered ghost-written by today's standards; some were dictated to an amanuensis; and some were authenticated as written by a fugitive slave. Adding further to differences between and among the items included in her survey, Starling finds a wide divergence in the length of materials considered as slave narratives; the materials vary from newspaper notices of a few paragraphs to book-length accounts of several hundred pages (1–49).

Few, if any, generalizations could cover such a variety of authorship and length over a period of more than two hundred years. Late eighteenth- and early nineteenth-century narratives are significantly different from antebellum narratives if only because of changes in the economic and historical context. Antebellum narratives are distinct from postbellum narratives, and the twentieth-century Federal Writers Project Slave Narrative Collection interviews are noticeably different from all of the preceding works. Consequently, sub-genres have become a necessary and convenient way to account for differences based on authorship, length of the composition, period of composition, and thematic focus.

Within these sub-genres critics generally have given an important position to the self-authored slave narratives written and published between 1830 and 1865. According to the *Oxford English Dictionary,* in its initial sense—"that part of a deed or document which contains a statement of the relevant or essential facts"—the term *narrative* entered English usage from the Scottish. In colonial American and eighteenth-century British literature narrative was applied to a variety of autobiographical accounts which emphasized the factuality of significant experiences in the life of the autobiographer, such as spiritual conversion, Indian captivity, or criminal confession, whether those accounts were attributed to whites or blacks. Thus narratives were not meant as complete autobiographies; instead, they foregrounded an ordeal—a turning point—in the life of the individual. By the antebellum period slave narratives had become a recognizable autobiographical form: a fact-based tale of a life beginning in slavery and ending in freedom. The antebellum narratives represented the crystallization of trends begun in the late eighteenth century, and the conventions of these antebellum narratives, especially those established by the written experiences of Douglass and Jacobs, have become generic standards.

The antebellum slave narratives were written amidst the heat of the slavery debate when the North and South represented, at least rhetorically, polar opposites. Many of these antebellum narratives share structures and metaphors that reflect this dichotomy: the narrators awaken to their physical and psychological enslavement in the South, resolve to be free, then, using various individual means, escape to the North where they end their quests in freedom. This physical and psychological quest constitutes the vertical trope which many critics consider central to the antebellum narrative. In a country geographically and politically divided by the presence or absence of slavery, fugitive slaves had a unique rhetorical status for Northern audiences as witness-participants, a status that gave self-authored texts a special authority. Contributing further to the authority of self-authorship, with its implications of literacy and authenticity, was the publication of some narratives as book-length, self-contained texts, which gave the author the space necessary for a more individualized, thematic treatment of the subject. Indeed, the antebellum period marks a distinct era in the production of book-length texts authored by ex-slaves.

Henry Bibb enters African American autobiographical literature as the author of one of these distinctive antebellum works. Bibb was born a slave in 1815 in Shelby County, Kentucky, and as a youth he was frequently hired out as a house servant to the owners of the plantations and farms in the area. Unlike so many slaves, Bibb rarely seemed daunted in his attempts to escape slavery. He began short-term, temporary running away, or maroonage, at the age of ten so that by the time he became a young man he had mastered what he refers to in his *Life and Adventures* as the "art of running away." Bibb was about twenty-two years old when he made his first flight to free territory in the North during the winter of 1837; but over the next four years he returned to the South, was recaptured, and escaped on five other occasions (two of these escape attempts were unsuccessful) before settling in the Detroit, Michigan area and joining the antislavery movement as a lecturer.

The details of the oral narrative which Bibb then began to relate from the antislavery lecture platform were so different from the typical ex-slave's account that in 1845 the Detroit Liberty Party established a special committee to investigate and verify the events of Bibb's incredible story of escape from and return to the South. Around the same time he was delivering lectures exposing the evils of slavery Bibb became actively involved in antislavery political work with the Liberty and Free Soil Parties, primarily in Michigan and New York.

Bibb's proficiency in the "art of running away" and in attacking slavery are more than enough to merit a modern reader's attention. However, the current critical attention given to the narratives of Frederick Douglass and Harriet Jacobs as the models for and the best examples of male and female slave narratives increases the urgency of giving greater attention to Bibb's life's story. On the one hand, Douglass all but eliminates any discussion of his wife so that he may present himself as a lone male escaping slavery and becoming the model of a black self-made man. Douglass's account has led to charges from some contemporary, often feminist, critics that he and other male narrators largely ignore slave women or treat them as objects in the development of their stories of male individualism. On the other hand, Jacobs presents herself in contrast to the middle-class ideal of proper behavior for a young, unmarried woman to demonstrate that slavery has stolen her opportunity to marry and establish a respectable family. Jacobs, under the pseudonym Linda Brent, decides to have children by an unmarried white man, without the sanction of marriage, as a compromise between coerced adultery with her master and marriage to a free black carpenter, which her master forbids. In addition, her narrative moves away from Douglass's individualism and develops the importance of a community of women, both black and white, in slavery and in freedom. When the narratives of Douglass and Jacobs are considered in isolation from other slave narratives they avoid or eliminate the story of slave marriage and the exploration of the metaphors that such a marriage suggests. In his study of black autobiography, *My Father's Shadow,* David Dudley summarizes current thinking by using Douglass and Jacobs as models for a tradition of black autobiographical writing: "Black men still tend to view themselves as isolated characters striving alone to make their way in life, while women tend to see themselves in relation to others, particularly to their mothers, to their children, and to other women" (31).

In contrast to both Douglass and Jacobs, Bibb shares

with his audience the story of his courtship, his slave marriage, and his divorce. According to his *Life and Adventures,* in 1833 Bibb exchanged wedding vows with Malinda, a slave on a neighboring Kentucky plantation, and together they had a daughter, Mary Frances, in 1835. This slave family, unrecognized by law or organized religion, becomes central to the form and content of Bibb's written narrative, as it had been for his earlier oral version of his life's story on the antislavery lecture platform. For instance, the suspense in Bibb's story depends on whether he will rescue his family, not on whether he will successfully escape to the North. Because of his concern for his slave family, Bibb rewrites the symbolic, and seemingly irreversible, transformation in the conventional linear plot of the fugitive's journey from slave in the South to free man in the North. After he reached the free North, Bibb returned to Kentucky to rescue his family; on several of these returns, he was recaptured before escaping again.

After one of these unsuccessful attempts to free his family from slavery in Kentucky, Bibb reports that he was sold with his wife and child to a plantation in Louisiana in 1839. Although he tried to escape from Louisiana with his family, they were recaptured; Bibb was then separated from Malinda and Mary Frances and sold to a band of traveling gamblers. They in turn sold him to an American Indian from whom Bibb eventually escaped to the North once again. Consequently, when Bibb joined the antislavery movement in Detroit, Michigan, he did so with a personal mission: to raise the money necessary to purchase his wife and child and reestablish his family in freedom. In the closing chapters of his narrative, however, after several agents have failed to locate his wife and family, Bibb recounts that he grew restless and returned as far south as

Madison, Indiana, a small town across the river from friends and relatives in Kentucky. At that time he was informed that his wife had been sold from the Louisiana plantation where he had last seen her and that for the last three years she had been living as the mistress of her new owner. At this point in his narrative Bibb declares himself divorced from his slave wife, just as he had entered marriage through a vow rather than a legal ceremony.

After his self-declared divorce Bibb returned to his antislavery labors in the Detroit area. Through his lecturing and participation in the antebellum black convention movement he became acquainted with other black activists such as Frederick Douglass and Martin Delany, a free black who was active in antislavery and black emigration projects. In 1847 Bibb met and began a courtship of Mary E. Miles, who was born a free woman in Massachusetts. After graduating from the Normal School in Albany, New York, she went on to make a reputation as an educator in Massachusetts, Pennsylvania, and New York, in addition to working in the antislavery movement. In June 1848 Bibb legally and formally married her. As a couple Henry and Mary Bibb continued to work together in a wide range of antislavery and racial-uplift activities.

In 1849 Bibb published the poignant story of his doomed attempt to have both freedom and family. Although his narrative was popular with northern audiences, Bibb and his wife emigrated to Canada after the passage of a stronger Fugitive Slave Law in 1850 because of his concerns for his safety. Henry and Mary Bibb became leaders of the growing fugitive slave community in Canada and strong advocates of education. Mary returned to her profession as a teacher and opened a school in their home for the children of fugitive slaves. Unfortunately, the school grew so large and so rapidly that it was plagued by financial problems. The Bibbs also supported emigration to Canada in speeches and in print; not surprisingly, Bibb was one of the major advocates and sponsors of a black emigration convention held in Toronto in 1852. Of course, they also aided fugitive slaves with advice and sometimes with room and board as they arrived in Canada. As a culmination of these activities, Bibb and his wife worked diligently to establish the Refugee Home Society as a model settlement for fugitives, and encouraged moral uplift through their support of temperance and the Methodist church.

In 1851 Bibb was able to reach a wider audience with his ideas when he became editor and publisher of the biweekly *Voice of the Fugitive,* the first black Canadian newspaper. In his editorials Bibb defended the black community against the all-too-frequently racist portrayals found in some mainstream Canadian newspapers; moreover, he strongly advocated land ownership and agricultural production for blacks because he felt that these were the means by which they could truly become independent. In addition, Bibb felt that ex-slaves usually had already acquired skill in agricultural production during their enslavement.

Bibb's activities in Canada did not escape challenges from other black activists. Indeed, the final years of his short life were troubled by a bitter dispute with Mary Ann Shadd Cary, a free black woman who had also emigrated to Canada after the Fugitive Slave Law was strengthened in 1850. The contrasts in the views of the two made conflict all but inevitable. Bibb was the editor of the *Voice of the Fugitive,* which advocated that blacks control their own affairs; Cary was the editor of the more integrationist

Provincial Freeman. Their differences in outlook were notable in their editorial positions. Bibb favored independent and separate growth for the black community; Cary
favored an integration of blacks into Canadian society.
Bibb favored soliciting funds to build the black community; Cary rejected such solicitations as begging. Bibb saw
emigration as a temporary measure and looked forward
to an eventual return to the United States; Cary saw
Canada as a permanent home.

In October of 1853 the printing press and office of the
Voice of the Fugitive were destroyed by a fire which Bibb
suspected was the work of arsonists. Despite Bibb's hopes
of reestablishing the enterprise, he never printed another
issue. Bibb died at the age of thirty-nine in August of the
following year, ending a career dedicated to serving the
African American community.

II

*Narrative of the Life and Adventures of Henry Bibb, an
American Slave; Written by Himself* is a complex autobiographical statement within the antebellum slave narrative
genre. Bibb gives his *Life and Adventures* a formal and thematic focus by demonstrating his desire to have both freedom and a family. This desire gives his story the recursive
pattern of escape and return, which is a significant varia-
tion from the conventional linear pattern of escape and
transformation into a free man. As his life's story unfolds,
however, he realizes that he can only have a slave wife and
family if he remains a slave himself. Thus, closure comes
to his story with his declaration of divorce from his slave
wife and his legal marriage to a free black woman. As in
any autobiographical statement, Bibb, as narrator, knows

how his story will end and at several points he reveals this foreknowledge. Nevertheless, Bibb adds poignancy to his story by allowing himself, as the protagonist within his narration, to discover, along with his reader, how events will unfold. This relationship between Bibb as narrator and Bibb as protagonist within his narration gives his story a striking tone which vacillates between renunciation of slavery and nostalgia for the slave community, which he exemplifies through his relationship to his slave wife and child.

By writing a book-length autobiographical statement, Bibb allowed himself the space to fully explore and shape the story of his ordeal with slavery. The *Life and Adventures'* twenty chapters can be divided into stages revealing the development of the conflict between family and freedom. In chapters one through three Bibb builds his relationship to the slave community, culminating in his marriage and family. In chapters four through seven he establishes his pattern of recursively escaping to the North and returning to Kentucky to rescue his wife and daughter. In chapters eight through twelve Bibb is reunited with his family, but having his slave family requires that they all be sold to the Deep South, where Bibb makes one futile attempt to escape with Malinda and Mary Frances. While he tells of his escape from the Deep South and his experiences as the slave of a Native American in chapters thirteen through sixteen, this successful escape comes only after he has been sold away from his family. In chapter seventeen Bibb begins his career as an abolitionist whose major motive is to raise enough money to purchase his family. Chapter eighteen marks the climax of the *Life and Adventures* as Bibb relates his divorce from Malinda. The final two chapters are anticlimactic: Bibb tells of his marriage to Mary Miles and makes his closing statements.

The first three chapters of Bibb's *Life and Adventures* could easily be read as a loosely organized account of more or less random events in the life of a young Kentucky slave. Bibb writes of maroonage—temporary running away to the surrounding countryside—conjure, the courtship of young women, and slave marriage and family. When these chapters are read in terms of developing the theme of freedom and family, however, they show Bibb introducing basic elements that will grow to establish his personal conflict with slavery, marriage, and freedom.

In the opening chapters Bibb recounts a number of strategies he developed as a youth to adjust to life as a slave, for, despite interjections by the narrator about the importance of freedom, he only runs away to the North after his marriage. In chapter one he learns that experience is education for a rural or plantation slave; he gains experience by being hired out several times. In addition, he claims to have an intuitive desire to be free: "This seemed to be a part of my nature; it was first revealed to me by the inevitable laws of nature's God" (17). Spurred by his natural inclination and relying on his experiences working in various areas of rural Kentucky, Bibb begins maroonage at the age of ten as an attempt to deal with the harsh treatment a young slave encountered. When experience shows him that running away to the surrounding forests is an effective temporary relief from mistreatment, he "learned the art of running away to perfection" (15).

In the first chapter Bibb also begins to shape the conflict between slavery and family. In lamenting his youthful condition, Bibb adds domestic rights to the political rights denied to the oxymoron American slave: "I believed then, as I believe now, that every man has a right to wages for his labor; *a right to his own wife and children;* a right to liberty and the pursuit of happiness; and a right to worship God according to the dictates of his own conscience" (17, italics mine). Despite the use of then and now to join narrator and protagonist, Bibb had neither met nor married Malinda at this point in his story; the only time markers in the chapter are his birth year, 1815, and the year he first temporarily ran away, 1825.

In chapter two Bibb relates the denial of religious rights and literacy to slaves as he recalls the failed attempt of a poor white woman to teach a Bible school for the slaves. Without such moral guidance the slaves adjust to their condition by amusing themselves with hunting, wrestling, drinking, and other diversions. Like Bibb they are by experience and by nature disinclined to practice the slave owner's religion of obedience. In describing these adjustments Bibb introduces a second technique he used to ameliorate the cruelties of slavery—the art of conjure. Noting that at age eighteen he was fond of visiting neighboring plantations, Bibb relates his experiences with conjure as a means of avoiding punishment.

In one of these episodes he stays too long visiting and must choose between the arts of conjure and maroonage to adjust to his situation as a slave. Bibb states, "I had a strong notion of running off, to escape being flogged, but was advised by a friend to go to one of those conjurers, who could prevent me from being flogged" (26). Youthfully impressed when he is not beaten on this occasion, he puts the conjure to more extreme tests by staying away for a longer visit and "talking saucy" to his disgruntled owner. In these cases the conjure fails to protect him, as does a potion prepared by another conjure man; in fact, Bibb exaggerates these episodes into hyperbolic failures to adjust to slavery. Significantly, in both cases he stresses avoiding punishment, not escape. As narrator, he then asserts the experiences reinforce his belief that "running away was the most effectual way by which a slave could escape cruel punishment" (28). As protagonist, however, he will return to conjure to facilitate his desires in courtship.

As his interest in courtship develops, Bibb brings together experience, conjure, courtship, and adjusting to slavery—the seemingly disparate and episodic elements of his first two chapters. In this way Bibb brings together the attractions of the slave community, as he sees them as an eighteen-year-old, and the means available to engage those attractions within the slave system, as he describes them as narrator. Unlike Douglass, who brings male slaves together to read and plot escape, Bibb's protagonist finds attractions within the slave community that turn him from escape. As he did with the potions to prevent floggings, Bibb deflates and dismisses the love charms of the conjurers hyperbolically. The charms not only fail to make him attractive to the women he desires, his comic misuse of them also causes the women to reject him.

In chapter three Bibb more fully combines these elements in his description of Malinda and the tensions created by his desire to join with her in a family. While he attempts to adjust to his limitations as a young male slave through conjure and the society of young women in chapters one and two, in chapter three he is himself controlled and conjured by "the fascinating charms of a female, who gradually won my attention from an object so high as that of liberty" (33). Bibb's choice of words—he uses "charms" to describe his attraction to Malinda again a paragraph later—conflates conjure and women, combining both in the person of his future slave wife. Significantly for later events, by the time he introduces Malinda, he has discredited conjure as superstition and women as obstacles to freedom. In this way the narrator anticipates and prepares for the eventual story of his divorce, since he claims to have learned that running away is the only solution.

Given the importance of literacy in Douglass's *Narrative* and in the antebellum slave-narrative genre, Bibb's decision to present his enchantment by Malinda as a parody of reading is an insightful, perhaps brilliant, revision of a major slave narrative convention. Nostalgia for Malinda is obvious when he recounts their mutual attraction as a "reading," but for a future fugitive slave he is exploring the wrong source:

> That Malinda loved me above all others on earth, no one could deny. I could *read* it by the warm reception with which the dear girl always met me, and treated me in her mother's house. I could *read* it by the warm and affectionate shake of the hand, and gentle smile upon her lovely cheek. I could *read* it by her always giving me the preference of her company; by her pressing invitations to visit even in opposition to her mother's will. I could *read* it in the language of her bright and sparkling eye, *penciled* by the unchanging finger of nature, that spake but could not lie. (34–35, italics mine)

While this romanticized literacy has a nostalgic charm for the protagonist, the narrator immediately returns the reader to the more important literacy of letters: "But oh! that I had only then been enabled to have seen as I do now, or to have *read* the following slave code, which is but a stereotyped law of American slavery" (35, italics mine). By listing pertinent slave laws, Bibb renounces his memory of courtship as a romanticized illusion of literacy. Retrospectively the narrator points out what time and experience have taught him: Slaves cannot legally marry, they live "in an open state of adultery, never having been married according to the laws of the State" (38).

Since Bibb can not legally sanction his marriage and he mentions no religious sanction, he and Malinda enter marriage through an informal exchange of vows. After their marriage he makes several references to the tension between his nostalgia for his slave wife and renunciation of slave marriage as an obstacle to freedom. In addition to his contrasts of the romantic literacy of his wife's charms with the verbal literacy of slave law, and their oral contract of marriage with the oxymorons of slave wife and family, Bibb also juxtaposes their matrimonial visiting on the plantation with running away to Canada. The narrator is, in fact, nostalgic even as he retrospectively renounces the marriage: "I often look back to that period *even now* as one of the most happy seasons of my life" (41, italics mine). However, the narrator also stresses renunciation in unequivocal passages: "If ever there was one act of my life while a slave, that I have to lament over it is that of being a father and a husband of slaves" (44).

Chapter three ends with Bibb's rationale for his first decision to escape alone, which initiates his recursive narrative pattern of escape and return. Despite the retrospective commentary of the narrator, until this point in his life running away has been Bibb's short-term attempt to ameliorate his condition as a slave. Although forced to witness his wife's exposure to the insults and abuse of slave drivers and overseers, the situation finally becomes unbearable with the birth and abuse of his daughter, Mary Frances, which forces Bibb into a new maturity. She turns his attention once more to running away; only now Canada, not the surrounding forest, is his destination. While Malinda's suffering concerns him greatly, Bibb's culpability for bringing another female into the same suffering causes him even greater grief, making him aware that as a husband and father he either has to escape from or collaborate with slavery; he finds no strategy for adjustment.

Given the foreknowledge of his story's conclusion, the narrator realizes that even as he constructs Malinda as his nostalgic metaphor for the charms and attractions of the slave community, he must eventually relate his divorce from her. Such a break could be read as a total condemnation of all that slavery includes—not only the exploitation of his liberty and labor, but also those who nurtured and suffered with him. Through Mary Frances, he forges an unbreakable link to that community. As Bibb notes, "I *was* a husband and *am* the father of slaves who are still left to linger out their days in hopeless bondage" (35, italics mine). While his verb tense shift anticipates his divorce and his continuing relationship with his daughter, he also elaborates his link to the slave community by conflating his wife and daughter. According to Bibb, Mary Frances is "the very image of her mother," and he predicts that she will share her mother's fate of physical and sexual abuse (44). In closing chapter three Bibb virtually replaces Malinda as wife with Mary Frances by his play on a quotation from Genesis, in which Adam, the first husband, speaks of Eve, the first wife and mother: "[Mary Frances] is bone of my bone, and flesh of my flesh; poor unfortunate child" (44). With this present tense allusion, Bibb also creates a domestic bond that cannot be broken by a declarative act as he does with the dissolution of his slave marriage.

While Bibb uses the opening chapters to introduce the tension between slavery, marriage, and freedom, he uses the next four chapters to act out these tensions as he recursively moves between the South and the North, attempting to have both his freedom and his family. Although Bibb and Malinda had discussed running away to Canada together as soon as possible, after three years of marriage he decides that he must "forsake friends and neighbors, wife and child, or consent to live and die a slave" (47). In fact, as he prepares to leave on Christmas Day of 1837, he does not inform Malinda that he is escaping to the North or that he plans to return to rescue her and his daughter, although the narrator assures the reader that he is only leaving his family to "go into a foreign country for a season" (43). Bibb chooses the Christmas season for his escape because a significant number of slaves were allowed to leave their home plantations and hire out their time to earn cash; many escaping slaves used the freedom of movement granted for such work or holiday leisure to cover the first days of their absence. Taking advantage of his owner's and his wife's assumptions that he is going to find work during the Christmas season, Bibb flees the South for Canada. In this initial escape to the North Bibb reinforces the conflict between marriage and slavery by presenting Malinda as an obstacle to his escape: "Had Malinda known my intention at that time, it would not have been possible for me to have got away, and I might have this day been a slave" (47). Bibb does not clarify this characterization.

Once he leaves Kentucky Bibb has relatively few problems crossing the Ohio River into Indiana and traveling from there to Cincinnati. With the aid of free blacks he continues on his way to Canada (50). On the journey he also learns of abolitionists for "the first time in [his] life" (51). Instead of going on to Canada that winter, Bibb stops at Perrysburgh, Ohio, where he found "quite a settlement of colored people, many of whom were fugitive slaves"

(55). Perhaps his contact with other fugitives reminds Bibb of his familial responsibilities because, after spending the winter as a woodchopper, he abandons the idea of proceeding to Canada and makes his first return to Kentucky to attempt to rescue his family in May of 1838. Although he and Malinda are temporarily reunited and make plans to escape together, they are unable to put their plan into action because Malinda is carefully watched: her owner fears that she will follow Bibb on her own initiative, rather than waiting for his return. After several weeks of waiting for an opportunity to escape together, the Bibbs develop just such a plan. In June of 1838 Bibb and Malinda resolve that he will go to Cincinnati and wait for her and Mary Frances to follow him in a week or two.

Bibb is betrayed to slave catchers in Cincinnati and is temporarily recaptured while waiting for his family; however, when he is brought back to Louisville, on his way to the Bedford, Kentucky, plantation of William Gatewood, he escapes from his jailer. Bibb then secretly returns to Gatewood's plantation and again plots to escape with his family. Because of Bibb's growing reputation as a runaway, and because of his owner's fears that he has returned to the area, however, Malinda is being watched even more closely. By the fall of 1838 they again resolve that Bibb will return to Ohio and that Malinda and Mary Frances will follow him after the excitement of his return and failed attempt to rescue his family has abated. Waiting eight or nine months in Ohio without hearing from his wife, Bibb returns to Kentucky a third time in July of 1839. After again making plans to escape with his family, Bibb's recursive adventures are stalled when he is betrayed by slaves, and he and his family are sold to a trader who takes them to the Deep South.

During the recursive movements of these chapters Bibb carefully develops the conflict between marriage and freedom. In this development, Malinda becomes clearly associated with adjustment to slavery. Each time he is temporarily recaptured, the slave catchers assure Bibb that he will not be punished or sold; instead they promise that he will be reunited with his wife and child if he gives up running away (64, 65). The association of Malinda with adjustment to slavery is reinforced further by Bibb's failure to give Malinda's explanations for her inability to follow him to the North as planned. Twice Bibb gives her money and instructions and waits in the North for her to follow him. In neither case does he relate her explanation for not following through with those plans. By the end of chapter seven an inability to reach free territory has become an element of Bibb's characterization of Malinda, a characterization that culminates in their abortive attempt to escape together in chapter eleven.

Bibb's returns to the South constantly threaten his precarious status as a fugitive. By returning to Kentucky Bibb risks reenslavement; when he is recaptured, he reverts from free man to reenslaved man. His mother's and wife's reactions to his reappearances are Bibb's clearest indication of the magnitude of this reversal. During his first return in the summer of 1838, Bibb is fortunate to find his wife and daughter spending the night at his mother's residence. On their seeing him again, Bibb remarks, "They never expected to see me again in this life" (58). Bibb makes this retransformation from free man to slave even clearer when he describes the reaction to his second return in the fall of 1838: "the raising of a dead body from the grave could not have been more surprising to any one than my arrival" (84). In both cases, the move from Northern freedom to Southern slavery takes on the magnitude of the irreversible transformation from life to death.

In chapter eight Bibb begins the account of his movement from the allegedly mild slavery of Kentucky, an upper southern state, to the harsher slavery of Louisiana. Once Bibb is recaptured his owner sells the family of three to a slave trader who is gathering a coffle of slaves to sell in New Orleans. Reinforcing his association of Malinda and Mary Frances with the people in slavery—people he retrospectively longs for when free but whom he must renounce or be enslaved—Bibb presents the reunion with his wife and child as a movement to the South rather than the hoped for movement North. Thematically, Bibb presents his desire for his slave family as such a contradiction and impossibility that he can only find adequate terms of narrative expression by reversing the slave narrative's conventional vertical trope of movement from slavery in the South to freedom in the North.

Furthermore, as he and his family move toward Louisiana, Bibb is forced into closer and closer collaboration with the system of slavery so that he may maintain his family. During his stay in the Louisville jail and the trip downriver to Louisiana, Bibb foregoes opportunities to escape "for the sake of my wife and child who was with me" (100). It is also a paradoxical sign of Bibb's attachment to his wife and daughter when, after a few months in New Orleans, he is given the job of finding a purchaser for himself and his family, further accentuating a sense of forced collaboration with slavery. Significantly, few buyers are interested in purchasing Bibb, but many are anxious to buy Malinda. Indeed, it is only in conjunction with Malinda and Mary Frances—that is, as a family—that Bibb finds a purchaser. Bibb's forced collaboration with slavery continues with the family's Louisiana purchaser, Deacon Whitfield, who expects Bibb to take a leadership position as the overseer on his Red River plantation.

In his account of his and his family's purchase in the Deep South, Bibb notes that slave traders and owners rely on his ties to his family to harness his abilities to the service of the slave system, even though they are suspicious of his intelligence and suspect his desire for freedom. Bibb's wife and child are the sources of contradictory impulses. On one hand, they lead him to seek his and their freedom in the North. On the other hand, to enjoy a semblance of family life, he must accept the restraints of slavery on all of them and their family relations. Instead of escaping with them into freedom and domestic autonomy, his desire for family leads him further and further from physical and domestic freedom in the North, and deeper and deeper into slavery in the Deep South.

In the Louisiana section of the *Life and Adventures* Bibb makes a telling break from the sequential plot conventionally used in autobiography and especially in slave narratives. While the events of chapter eleven precede those of chapter twelve in Bibb's arrangement of his text, the events of chapter twelve occur earlier chronologically and help to determine both the events and their consequences in chapter eleven. Importantly, both chapters eleven and twelve deal with attempted escapes from Whitfield's plantation; one escape dramatizes Bibb's facility in the "art of running away" without his family while the other foregrounds his failure to escape with them.

The attempt to escape with his family is crucial to the *Life and Adventures* because it is Bibb's only account of an escape with his family and because he takes the episode out of the sequential flow of his story to emphasize its im-

portance. In his previous attempts to rescue his family
from Kentucky, vigilant whites forced them to attempt to
escape separately, with Bibb succeeding in reaching the
North and Malinda remaining in the South for unex-
plained reasons. Bibb's stated motive for running away in
chapter eleven is that, because he slips away to a prayer
meeting which Whitfield had forbidden him to attend,
Whitfield announces that Bibb will receive "500 lashes"
when he returns to the plantation. Malinda intercepts him
as he returns, however, and informs him of Whitfield's
plan to flog him. At this point Bibb decides to run away
alone, but because the jackass he steals to add speed to his
escape is uncooperative, he returns, gathers his family, and
attempts to escape with them on foot.

In sharp contrast to the characterization of his maroonage to escape punishment in chapter one when he
learns the "art of running away to perfection" (15), and
his lone escapes in 1837 and 1838, in chapter eleven the
narrator describes the joint attempt as doomed from the
outset. Even before relating their escape, he interjects
the hope that when they are caught Whitfield "might sell
us all, and perhaps to the same person" (122). Also, prior
to his account of their ten-day trek in the "swamps" and
"wilderness," the narrator gives advance notice that "it
was all in vain" (123). In earlier escapes from Kentucky
Bibb had little or no trouble crossing the Ohio River
alone; in this joint effort, however, Bibb and his family can
find no way to cross the Red River. Indeed, Bibb, who had
found his way to Canada earlier, admits that "most of the
time, while we were out, we were lost" (123). Moreover,
while lost they are, on one occasion, prey for wolves which
surround them at night. Although Bibb runs the wolves
away, the presence of wild animals in the episode under-

lines the depiction of himself as a lost, hungry, and concerned husband and parent.

Taken alone, chapter eleven shows that escape from the Deep South is extremely difficult; when chapter eleven is read in conjunction with chapter twelve, however, it becomes obvious that Bibb depicts his family as both worth facing wild animals for and as an obstacle to freedom. Chapter twelve begins with Bibb receiving a flogging after he and his family are recaptured, but in midchapter, Bibb somewhat offhandedly recalls: "I have omitted to state that this was the second time I had run away from [Whitfield]" (134). This first instance of running away largely accounts for the consequent harshness of Bibb's flogging and for his owner's consequent insistence on selling Bibb away from his family after the second attempt. While the escape with his family appears to simply follow Bibb's attendance at a prayer service, it is closely related to the prior escape.

In retroactive contrast to the hopelessness with which he describes himself and his family wandering for ten days in a Red River swamp in chapter eleven, Bibb and "an old slave by the name of Jack" decide "to take a tramp" together "for ill treatment" (135) in chapter twelve. The choice of the word "tramp" gives a lighthearted, frolicking quality to the onset of this episode, which the following events justify. For this tramp, Bibb has no sense of being lost or struggling in a "wilderness"; instead, he "was to be the pilot, while Jack was to carry the baggage and keep us in provisions" (135). A sense of organization and purposefulness dominates the episode and recalls for the reader the Bibb of the earlier chapters, the master of the "art of running away." Bibb and Jack are "bound for the city of Little Rock, State of Arkansas," they travel "by night and laid by in the day," and they are "guided by the unchangeable North Star" (135).

Both the details of chapters eleven and twelve and Bibb's telling them out of sequence emphasize the contrast between his well-planned escapade with Jack and the panicked anarchy of his failed attempt to escape with his family. Bibb and Jack even elude the slave-catching dogs during their tramp, but the dogs are inescapable in his attempt to run away (later) with Malinda and Mary Frances. When they are recaptured and returned to Whitfield, Bibb is given a light punishment—in contrast to the 500 lashes he receives when he and his family are recaptured—despite the fact that Malinda reveals his history of running away, because his owner blames Jack for persuading Bibb to take up his old habits. However, the overall effect of the contrast between the two episodes, as well as their placement in the narrative sequence, dramatizes Bibb's inability to successfully pursue freedom with his wife and daughter. His family domesticates him to the extent that the intrepid fugitive of chapter twelve is unable to function as a runaway when he must also function as a husband and father; by the same token, Malinda cannot run away as mother and wife. Domestic ties for slaves, though poignant, are thus presented as sources of control and adjustment within the slave system.

Once he is sold away from his family, Bibb's treatment as a slave becomes milder and milder. This more clement treatment is ironic. Bibb's Louisiana owner is a deacon in the Methodist church, but he has no qualms with harsh treatment or breaking up slave families. In contrast, Deacon Whitfield sells Bibb to a band of southern gamblers, or blacklegs, who try to buy his wife and child to keep the family together and who cry sympathetic tears as they watch Bibb's emotional separation from his family. As the gamblers' servant, Bibb has to perform only the light duties of driving a wagon and blacking boots. The gamblers even go so far as to give Bibb money and information about escaping. After the gamblers sell him to a Native American in the Indian Territory of Arkansas, Bibb continues to contrast Christian slaveholders with those who are less religious. Bibb functions more as a manager of his owner's wealth than as a slave; in fact, he finds this to be the mildest of all his experiences with slavery. Upon the death of this owner in 1840, Bibb escapes like the old master of the "art of running away" and finally returns to the North.

Once in the North, Bibb begins his public career as an abolitionist orator; thus Bibb re-creates his recursive experiences rhetorically in an oral narrative that provides several years of preparation for his written story. In contrast to his initial expectations and hopes, Bibb's narrative closure is not his escape and return to the North with his family but a final break with his family, which he recounts in chapter eighteen. Late in the fall of 1845, Bibb once again journeys southward, where he is informed by an unnamed "good authority" that his wife has been sold and that she is "living in a state of adultery with her master, and had been for the last three years" (188). Just as his marriage comes into existence through a declarative act, Bibb divorces Malinda by declaring her "theoretically and practically dead to me as a wife, for she was living in a state of adultery, according to the law of God and man" (189).

This declaration allows Bibb to pursue Mary E. Miles two years later, in 1847. In contrast to Malinda, "the dear girl" of his slave past, Miles is a "lady whom [he] had frequently heard very highly spoken of, for her activity and devotion to the anti-slavery cause, as well as her talents and learning, and benevolence in the cause of reforms, generally" (190–91). They are married in a religious ceremony, and Bibb finally enters into the kind of legally protected monogamy that he has sought from the beginning of the narrative. Bibb's characterization of Miles as a free, Northern, educated abolitionist underlines the contrast between his second wife and his more "enchanting" slave wife. Bibb resolves the tensions between freedom and family by divorcing the more vivacious slave woman who had kept him returning to the South, and marrying a phlegmatic, Northern free woman, who embodies the qualities he seeks in the North. Bibb effectively completes the plot of his *Life and Adventures* with chapter eighteen. For all practical purposes, chapters nineteen and twenty are commentaries on other parts of the *Life and Adventures* and do not move beyond the events of 1848 or amplify important prior events. In terms of Bibb's narrative structure, the final two chapters are clearly anticlimactic. Bibb's divorce from his slave wife and remarriage to a free black woman end the plot that began with the youthful protagonist's attempts to adjust to slavery through maroonage, conjure, courtship, and marriage.

III

A large measure of the significance of Henry Bibb's *Life and Adventures* derives from the centrality he gives to family relations. Family relations provide the key to the form and content of Bibb's life's story, and these relations explain his breaks from conventions and reader expectations for self-authored, book-length accounts written during the antebellum period. In *The Slave Narrative,*

Marion Wilson Starling places Bibb's differences from the conventional slave narratives in a completely different light. She points out that, when we disregard issues of authorship and publication, the majority of the antebellum stories of fugitive slaves that have been preserved in newspaper accounts and interviews involve the escape of families—that is, of husbands and wives, parents and children—rather than the stories of a lone unattached male, such as Frederick Douglass, William Wells Brown, James W. C. Pennington, and others. Starling goes on to make this cogent observation:

> Although about one-half of the separately published slave narratives of this period tell of their author's escape from slavery as young, unmarried men, the overwhelming majority of the total slave narratives of the period tell of the flight of whole families, of fathers going ahead on reconnoitering trips and braving incredible dangers, including probable death if caught, in their return trips to take their families to some "place" they had found for them. (30)

At least in this broad context, Bibb's *Life and Adventures* may be more representative of the concerns of antebellum African Americans than the more recognizable story of escape by a lone unattached male.

Because of the importance of family in the creation of his *Life and Adventures,* Bibb's plot has a distinctive recursive pattern as he moves back and forth between the South and North. Unlike the expected linear pattern of escape to the North and irreversible transformation into a free person, Bibb's recursive story emphasizes the importance of family because he risks his tenuous freedom again and again by returning to the South for futile attempts to rescue Malinda and Mary Frances. This interest in family also generates suspense in Bibb's account of his experiences. Conventionally, antebellum slave narratives are without genuine suspense: although narrators might express doubts about the success of their escapes, the publication of the narratives implicitly assures the reader of the narrators' freedom. Bibb's emphasis on the "art of running away," however, shifts the reader's attention from the guarantee of his escape to the suspense of whether he can successfully rescue his slave family.

Indeed, Bibb's knowledge that his slave marriage will fail is central to the complex relationship between Bibb as autobiographical narrator, who knows how past events lead to his divorce and remarriage, and Bibb as autobiographical hero, who must move through events before arriving at the narrator's level of awareness. This split between narrator and protagonist adds to the poignant tone of Bibb's story, as Bibb vacillates between nostalgia for the slave community, represented by his wife and daughter, and renunciation of the institution of slavery in an attempt to prepare his reading audience for his eventual divorce from his slave wife.

Bibb's emphasis on marriage and family also places his autobiographical work in a significant dialogue with other nineteenth century works of African American fiction. If the slave narratives are the wellspring for African American literature, then Bibb's story needs to be compared with William Wells Brown's *Clotel, or, The President's Daughter;* Frederick Douglass's *The Heroic Slave;* Martin Delaney's *Blake, or, The Huts of America;* and postbellum writers of sentimental fiction such as Frances Watkins Harper and Pauline Hopkins. All of these authors share a concern for the importance of marriage and family, and frequently, this concern is presented as leaving freedom in the North on a quest to rescue enslaved family members in the South.

In terms of more recent literature, there are intriguing

possibilities in comparing Bibb's *Life and Adventures* to Toni Morrison's critically acclaimed novel, *Beloved.* In telling her story of slave marriage and family, Morrison creates a novel that has significant parallels with Bibb's *Life and Adventures;* both works highlight the importance of coming to terms with forces from the past that cannot be ignored. *Beloved* is in several ways an artistic culmination of Bibb's recursive narrative design and his thematic focus on the conflicts and complexities involved in moving from slavery to freedom. For Bibb, the recursion and conflict are primarily presented in external, physical terms: his vacillation between freedom and family is represented geographically as he repeatedly moves from South to North to South. Morrison's great achievement is taking the physical, largely externalized conflict between personal freedom and community and exploring its internal psychological and spiritual depths. Although Sethe is the central focus of the novel, her conflict is elaborated upon and amplified by the subplots involving similar conflicts within Baby Suggs, Paul D., Stamp Paid, and Ella. Rather than physical movement and the externalized possibility of freedom, Morrison makes the struggle for freedom an internal conflict with an internalized resolution, although the figure of Beloved is open to interpretation on a physical or spiritual level.

The remainder of this edition contains the complete text of Bibb's *Life and Adventures.* The original *Life and Adventures* has, on its opening page, a likeness of Bibb that was created by Patrick Reason, a Haitian artist who had emigrated to the New York area. In the engraving Bibb holds a copy of the Bible, which reflects his religious enthusiasm and recalls a similar posture by Gustavus Vassa in his influential eighteenth-century autobiography, *The Interesting Narrative of the Life of Olaudah Equiano, or Gustavus Vassa, The African; Written by Himself* (1789). There is also a smaller depiction of Bibb running away from pursuers. Both of these images appear on the cover of this volume. While these images make reference to Bibb as abolitionist speaker and fugitive, the frontispiece shows Bibb taking leave of Malinda and Mary Frances and seems to set in motion the suspense of whether he can rescue them as the reader opens the text. Other images are scattered throughout the *Life and Adventures*. The drawing of Bibb fighting off wild animals while protecting his family during an attempted escape is notable (125); William Wells Brown had a depiction of the same scene made as a part of a diorama that he used to raise funds during his stay in England during the 1850s.

The text itself can be divided into several parts. Lucius C. Matlack's introduction contains his thoughts on Bibb's *Life and Adventures,* some of the authenticating documents from the 1845 Liberty Party Committee's investigation of Bibb's oral narrative, and Matlack's commentary on those documents. In the author's preface Bibb explains why he has chosen to publish a written narrative. There are twenty chapters in the narrative proper. In these chapters Bibb also includes more authenticating materials in the form of a letter from his former owner, his response, and documents generated by the Liberty Party in commissioning him as an antislavery agent.

In an appendix I have included a sample of Bibb's writing before and after his *Life and Adventures* was published. I have selected Bibb's letter to James G. Birney because it shows his concern for his slave family, his response to those who doubted his credibility, and because it helps to clarify the issue of Matlack's role as editor of Bibb's text. I have also included a Prospectus for the *Voice of the Fugitive* because it summarizes Bibb's writing career after the publication of the *Life and Adventures*. In addition, I have included editorials on racial prejudice, education, and the Refugee Home Society—all of which represent significant interests of both Bibb and his wife. This edition closes with a chronology of important events described in the *Life and Adventures* and in Bibb's life after its publication and a bibliography of works related to slave narratives generally and Bibb's *Life and Adventures* specifically.

LIFE AND ADVENTURES

OF

HENRY BIBB,

NARRATIVE

OF THE

LIFE AND ADVENTURES

OF

HENRY BIBB,

AN AMERICAN SLAVE

WRITTEN BY HIMSELF.

WITH

AN INTRODUCTION

BY LUCIUS C. MATLACK.

NEW YORK:
PUBLISHED BY THE AUTHOR; 5 SPRUCE STREET.
1850.

INTRODUCTION.

FROM the most obnoxious substances we often see spring forth, beautiful and fragrant, flowers of every hue, to regale the eye, and perfume the air. Thus, frequently, are results originated which are wholly unlike the cause that gave them birth. An illustration of this truth is afforded by the history of American Slavery.

Naturally and necessarily, the enemy of literature, it has become the prolific theme of much that is profound in argument, sublime in poetry, and thrilling in narrative. From the soil of slavery itself have sprung forth some of the most brilliant productions, whose logical levers will ultimately upheave and overthrow the system. Gushing fountains of poetic thought, have started from beneath the rod of violence, that will long continue to slake the feverish thirst of humanity outraged, until swelling to a flood it shall rush with wasting violence over the ill-gotten heritage of the oppressor. Startling incidents authenticated, far excelling fiction in their touching pathos, from the pen of self-emancipated slaves, do now exhibit slavery in such revolting aspects, as to secure the execrations of all good men, and become a monument more enduring than marble, in testimony strong as sacred writ against it.

Of the class last named, is the narrative of the life of Henry Bibb, which is equally distinguished as a revolting portrait of the hideous slave system, a thrilling narrative of individual suffering, and a triumphant vindication of the slave's manhood and mental dignity. And all this is associated with unmistakable traces of originality and truthfulness.

To many, the elevated style, purity of diction, and easy flow of language, frequently exhibited, will appear unaccountable and contradictory, in view of his want of early mental culture

But to the thousands who have listened with delight to his speeches on anniversary and other occasions, these same traits will be noted as unequivocal evidence of originality. Very few men present in their written composition, so perfect a transcript of their style as is exhibited by Mr. Bibb.

Moreover, the writer of this introduction is well acquainted with his handwriting and style. The entire manuscript I have examined and prepared for the press. Many of the closing pages of it were written by Mr. Bibb in my office. And the whole is preserved for inspection now. An examination of it will show that no alteration of sentiment, language or style, was necessary to make it what it now is, in the hands of the reader. The work of preparation for the press was that of orthography and punctuation merely, an arrangement of the chapters, and a table of contents—little more than falls to the lot of publishers generally.

The fidelity of the narrative is sustained by the most satisfactory and ample testimony. Time has proved its claims to truth. Thorough investigation has sifted and analysed every essential fact alleged, and demonstrated clearly that this thrilling and eloquent narrative, though stranger than fiction, is undoubtedly true.

It is only necessary to present the following documents to the reader, to sustain this declaration. For convenience of reference, and that they may be more easily understood, the letters will be inserted consecutively, with explanations following the last.

The best preface to these letters, is, the report of a committee appointed to investigate the truth of Mr. Bibb's narrative as he has delivered it in public for years past.

REPORT

OF THE UNDERSIGNED, COMMITTEE APPOINTED BY THE DETROIT LIBERTY ASSOCIATION TO INVESTIGATE THE TRUTH OF THE NARRATIVE OF HENRY BIBB, A FUGITIVE FROM SLAVERY, AND REPORT THEREON:

Mr. Bibb has addressed several assemblies in Michigan, and his narrative is generally known. Some of his hearers, among whom were Liberty men, felt doubt as to the truth of his statements. Respect for their scruples and the obligation of duty to the public induced the formation of the present Committee. The Committee entered on the duty confided to them, resolved on a searching scrutiny, and an unreserved publication of its result. Mr. Bibb acquiesced in the inquiry with a praiseworthy spirit. He attended before the Committee and gave willing aid to its object. He was subjected to a rigorous examination. Facts—dates—persons—and localities were demanded and cheerfully furnished. Proper inquiry—either by letter, or personally, or through the medium of friends was then made from every person, and in every quarter likely to elucidate the truth. In fact no test for its ascertainment, known to the sense or experience of the Committee, was omitted. The result was the collection of a large body of testimony from very diversified quarters. Slave owners, slave dealers, fugitives from slavery, political friends and political foes contributed to a mass of testimony, every part of which pointed to a common conclusion—the undoubted truth of Mr. Bibb's statements.

In the Committee's opinion no individual can substantiate the events of his life by testimony more conclusive and harmonious than is now before them in confirmation of Mr. Bibb. The main facts of his narrative, and many of the minor ones are corroborated beyond all question. No inconsistency has been disclosed nor anything revealed to create suspicion. The Committee have no hesitation in declaring their conviction that Mr. Bibb is amply sustained, and is entitled to public confidence and high esteem.

The bulk of testimony precludes its publication, but it is in the Committee's hands for the inspection of any applicant.

A. L. PORTER,
C. H. STEWART,
SILAS M. HOLMES.

DETROIT, *April* 22, 1845.   Committee.

From the bulk of testimony obtained, a part only is here introduced. The remainder fully corroborates and strengthens that.

[No. 1. An Extract.]   DAWN MILLS, FEB. 19th, 1845.
        CHARLES H. STEWART, ESQ.
MY DEAR BROTHER :

Your kind communication of the 13th came to hand yesterday. I have made inquiries respecting Henry Bibb which may be of service to you. Mr. Wm. Harrison, to whom you allude in your letter, is here. He is a respectable and worthy man—a man of piety. I have just had an interview with him this evening. He testifies, that he was well acquainted with Henry Bibb in Trimble County, Ky., and that he sent a letter to him by Thomas Henson, and got one in return from him. He says that Bibb came out to Canada some three years ago, and went back to get his wife up, but was betrayed at Cincinnati by a colored man—that he was taken to Louisville but got away—

was taken again and lodged in jail, and sold off to New Orleans, or he, (Harrison,) understood that he was taken to New Orleans. He testifies that Bibb is a Methodist man, and says that two persons who came on with him last Summer, knew Bibb. One of these, Simpson Young, is now at Malden. * * *
Very respectfully, thy friend,
HIRAM WILSON.

[No. 2.]   BEDFORD, TRIMBLE Co., KENTUCKY.
                                 March 4, 1845.
SIR:—Your letter under date of the 13th ult., is now before me, making some inquiry about a person supposed to be a fugitive from the South, " who is lecturing to your religious community on Slavery and the South."

I am pleased to inform you that I have it in my power to give you the information you desire. The person spoken of by you I have no doubt is Walton, a yellow man, who once belonged to my father, William Gatewood. He was purchased by him from John Sibly, and by John Sibly of his brother Albert G. Sibly, and Albert G. Sibly became possessed of him by his marriage with Judge David White's daughter, he being born Judge White's slave.

The boy Walton at the time he belonged to John Sibly, married a slave of my father's, a mulatto girl, and sometime afterwards solicited him to buy him ; the old man after much importuning from Walton, consented to do so, and accordingly paid Sibly eight hundred and fifty dollars. He did not buy him because he needed him, but from the fact that he had a wife there, and Walton on his part promising every thing that my father could desire.

It was not long, however, before Walton became indolent and neglectful of his duty; and in addition to this, he was guilty, as the old man thought, of worse offences. He watched his conduct more strictly, and found he was guilty of disposing of articles from the farm for his own use, and pocketing the money.

He actually caught him one day stealing wheat—he had conveyed one sack full to a neighbor and whilst he was delivering the other my father caught him in the very act.

He confessed his guilt and promised to do better for the future—and on his making promises of this kind my father was disposed to keep him still, not wishing to part him from his wife, for whom he professed to entertain the strongest affection. When the Christmas Holidays came on, the old man, as is usual in this country, gave his negroes a week Holiday. Walton, instead of regaling himself by going about visiting his colored friends, took up his line of march for her Britanic Majesty's dominions.

He was gone about two years I think, when I heard of him

in Cincinnati ; I repaired thither, with some few friends to aid me, and succeeded in securing him.

He was taken to Louisville, and on the next morning after our arrival there, he escaped, almost from before our face, while we were on the street before the Tavern. He succeeded in eluding our pursuit, and again reached Canada in safety.

Nothing daunted he returned, after a lapse of some twelve or eighteen months, with the intention, as I have since learned, of conducting off his wife and eight or ten more slaves to Canada.

I got news of his whereabouts, and succeeded in recapturing him. I took him to Louisville and together with his wife and child, (she going along with him at her owner's request,) sold hem. He was taken from thence to New Orleans—and from hence to Red River, Arkansas—and the next news I had of him he was again wending his way to Canada, and I suppose now is at or near Detroit.

In relation to his character, it was the general opinion here that he was a notorious liar, and a rogue. These things I can procure any number of respectable witnesses to prove.

In proof of it, he says his mother belonged to James Bibb, which is a lie, there not having been such a man about here, much less brother of Secretary Bibb. He says that Bibb's danghter married A. G. Sibly, when the fact is Sibly married Judge David White's daughter, aud his mother belonged to White also and is now here, free.

So you will perceive he is guilty of lying for no effect, and what might it not be supposed he would do where he could effect anything by it.

I have been more tedious than I should have been, but being anxious to give you his rascally conduct in full, must be my apology. You are at liberty to publish this letter, or make any use you see proper of it. If you do publish it, let me have a paper containing the publication—at any rate let me hear from you again.

Respectfully yours, &c.,
SILAS GATEWOOD.

To C. H. STEWART, ESQ.

[No. 3. An Extract.]   CINCINNATI, *March* 10, 1845.

MY DEAR SIR :—Mrs. Path, Nickens and Woodson did not see Bibb on his first visit, in 1837, when he staid with Job Dundy, but were subsequently told of it by Bibb. They first saw him in May, 1838. Mrs. Path remembers this date because it was the month in which she removed from Broadway to Harrison street, and Bibb assisted her to remove. Mrs. Path's garden adjoined Dundy's back yard. While engaged in digging up flowers, she was addressed by Bibb, who was staying with Dundy and who offered to dig them up for her. She hired

him to do it. Mrs. Dundy shortly after called cver and told
Mrs. Path that he was a slave. After that Mrs. Path took him
into her house and concealed him. While concealed, he as-
tonished his good protectress by his ingenuity in bottoming
chairs with cane. When the furniture was removed, Bibb in-
sisted on helping, and was, after some remonstrances, permitted.
At the house on Harrison street, he was employed for several
days in digging a cellar, and was so employed when seized on
Saturday afternoon by the constables. He held frequent con-
versations with Mrs. Path and others, in which he gave them
the same account which he has given you.

On Saturday afternoon, two noted slave-catching constables,
E. V. Brooks and O'Neil, surprised Bibb as he was digging in
the cellar. Bibb sprang for the fence and gained the top of it,
where he was seized and dragged back. They took him immediately before William Doty, a Justice of infamous notoriety
as an accomplice of kidnappers, proved property, paid charges
and took him away.

His distressed friends were surprised by his re-appearance
in a few days after, the Wednesday following, as they think.
He reached the house of Dr. Woods, (a colored man since de-
ceased,) before day-break, and staid until dusk. Mrs. Path,
John Woodson and others made up about twelve dollars for him.
Woodson accompanied him out of town a mile and bid him
"God speed." He has never been here since. Woodson and
Clark saw him at Detroit two years ago.

Yours truly,
WILLIAM BIRNEY.

[No. 4.]   LOUISVILLE, *March* 14, 1845.
MR. STEWART.—Yours of the 1st came to hand on the 13th inst
You wished me to inform you what became of a boy that was
in the work-house in the fall of '39. The boy you allude to
went by the name of Walton; he had ran away from Kentucky
some time before, and returned for his wife—was caught and sold
to Garrison; he was taken to Louisiana, I think—he was sold
on Red River to a planter. As Garrison is absent in the City
of New Orleans at this time, I cannot inform you who he was
sold to. Garrison will be in Louisville some time this Spring;
if you wish me, I will inquire of Garrison and inform you to
whom he was sold, and where his master lives at this time.

Yours,
W. PORTER.

[No. 5.]   BEDFORD, TRIMBLE COUNTY, KY
C. H. STEWART, ESQ.,
SIR.—I received your note on the 16th inst., and in accordance
with it I write you these lines. You stated that you would

wish to know something about Walton H. Bibb, and whether
he had a wife and child, and whether they were sold to New
Orleans. Sir, before I answer these inquiries, I should like to
know who Charles H. Stewart is, and why you should make
these inquiries of me, and how you knew who I was, as you are
a stranger to me and I must be to you. In your next if you
will tell me the intention of your inquiries, I will give you a
full history of the whole case.

I have a boy in your county by the name of King, a large
man and very black ; if you are acquainted with him, give him
my compliments, and tell him I am well, and all of his friends.
W. H. Bibb is acquainted with him.

I wait your answer.

Your most obedient,

March 17, 1845.   W. H. GATEWOOD

[No. 6.]   BEDFORD, KENTUCKY, *April* 6th, 1845.
     MR. CHARLES H. STEWART.

SIR :—Yours of the 1st March is before me, inquiring if one
Walton Bibb, a colored man, escaped from me at Louisville, Ky.,
in the Spring of 1839. To that inquiry I answer, he did. The
particulars are these : He ran off from William Gatewood some
time in 1838 I think, and was heard of in Cincinnati. Myself and
some others went there and took him, and took him to Louisville for sale, by the directions of his master. While there he
made his escape and was gone some time, I think about one
year or longer. He came back it was said, to get his wife and
child, so report says. He was again taken by his owner; he
together with his wife and child was taken to Louisville and
sold to a man who traded in negroes, and was taken by him to
New Orleans and sold with his wife and child to some man up
Red River, so I was informed by the man who sold him. He
then ran off and left his wife and child and got back, it seems,
to your country. I can say for Gatewood he was a good master, and treated him well. Gatewood bought him from a Mr.
Sibly, who was going to send him down the river. Walton, to
my knowledge, influenced Gatewood to buy him, and promised
if he would, never to disobey him or run off. Who he belongs
to now, I do not know. I know Gatewood sold his wife and
child at a great sacrifice, to satisfy him. If any other information is necessary I will give it, if required . You will please
write me again what he is trying to do in your country, or what
he wishes the inquiry from me for.

Yours, truly,

DANIEL S. LANE.

These letters need little comment. Their testimony combined is most harmonious and conclusive. Look at the points
established.

1. Hiram Wilson gives the testimony of reputable men now in Canada, who knew Henry Bibb as a slave in Kentucky.

2. Silas Gatewood, with a peculiar relish, fills three pages of foolscap, " being anxious to give his rascally conduct in full," as he says. But he vaults over the saddle and lands on the other side. His testimony is invaluable as an endorsement of Mr. Bibb's truthfulness. He illustrates all the essential facts of this narrative. He also labors to prove him deceitful and a liar.

Deceit in a slave, is only a slight reflex of the stupendous fraud practised by his master. And its indulgence has far more logic in its favor, than the ablest plea ever written for slave holding, under ever such peculiar circumstances. The attempt to prove Mr Bibb in the lie, is a signal failure, as he never affirmed what Gatewood denies. With this offset, the letter under notice is a triumphant vindication of one, whom he thought there by to injure sadly. As Mr. Bibb has most happily acknowledged the wheat, (see page 194,) I pass the charge of stealing by referring to the logic there used, which will be deemed convincing.

3. William Birney, Esq., attests the facts of Mr. Bibb's arrest in Cincinnati, and the subsequent escape, as narrated by him, from the declaration of eye witnesses.

4. W. Porter, Jailor, states that Bibb was in the work-house at Louisville, held and sold afterwards to the persons and at the places named in this volume.

5. W. H. Gatewood, with much Southern dignity, will answer no questions, but shows his relation to these matters by naming "King"—saying, "W. H. Bibb is acquainted with him," and promising "a full history of the case."

6. Daniel S. Lane, with remarkable straight-forwardness and stupidity, tells all he knows, and then wants to know what they ask him for. The writer will answer that question. He wanted to prove by two or more witnesses, the truth of his own statements ; which has most surely been accomplished.

Having thus presented an array of testimony sustaining the facts alleged in this narrative, the introduction will be concluded by introducing a letter signed by respectable men of

Detroit, and endorsed by Judge Wilkins, showing the high esteem in which Mr. Bibb is held by those who know him well where he makes his home. Their testimony expresses their present regard as well as an opinion of his past character. It is introduced here with the greatest satisfaction, as the writer is assured, from an intimate acquaintance with Henry Bibb, that all who know him hereafter will entertain the same sentiments toward him:

DETROIT, *MARCH* 10, 1845

The undersigned have pleasure in recommending Henry Bibb to the kindness and confidence of Anti-slavery friends in every State. He has resided among us for some years. His deportment, his conduct, and his christian course have won our esteem and affection. The narrative of his sufferings and more early life has been thoroughly investigated by a Committee appointed for the purpose. They sought evidence respecting it in every proper quarter, and their report attested its undoubted truth. In this conclusion we all cordially unite.

H. Bibb has for some years publicly made this narrative to assemblies, whose number cannot be told; it has commanded public attention in this State, and provoked inquiry. Occasionally too we see persons from the South, who knew him in early years, yet not a word or fact worthy of impairing its truth has reached us; but on the contrary, every thing tended to its corroboration.

Mr. Bibb's Anti-slavery eforts in this State have produced incalculable benefit. The Lord has blessed him into an instrument of great power. He has labored much, and for very inadequate compensation. Lucrative offers for other quarters did not tempt him to a more profitable field. His sincerity and disinterestedness are therefore beyond suspicion.

We bid him "God-speed," on his route. We bespeak for him every kind consideration. * * * *

H. HALLOCK,
President of the Detroit Lib. Association.
CULLEN BROWN, *Vice-President.*
S. M. HOLMES, *Secretary.*
J.D. BALDWIN,
CHARLES H. STEWART,
MARTIN WILSON,
WILLIAM BARNUM.

DETROIT, *Nov.* 11, 1845.

The undersigned, cheerfully concurs with Mr. Hallock and others in their friendly recommendation of Mr. Henry Bibb. The undersigned has known him for many months in the Sabbath School in this City, partly under his charge, and can certify to his correct deportment, and commend him to the sympathies of Christian benevolence.

ROSS WILKINS.

———

The task now performed, in preparing for the press and introducing to the public the narrative of Henry Bibb, has been one of the most pleasant ever required at my hands. And I conclude it with an expression of the hope that it may afford interest to the reader, support to the author in his efforts against slavery, and be instrumental in advancing the great work of emancipation in this country.

LUCIUS C. MATLACK

NEW YORK CITY, *JULY* 1st, 1849.

AUTHOR'S PREFACE

This work has been written during irregular intervals, while I have
been travelling and laboring for the emancipation of my enslaved countrymen. The reader will remember that I make no pretension to literature; for I can truly say, that I have been educated in the school of
adversity, whips, and chains. Experience and observation have been my
principal teachers, with the exception of three weeks schooling which I
have had the good fortune to receive since my escape from the "grave
yard of the mind," or the dark prison of human bondage. And nothing
but untiring perseverance has enabled me to prepare this volume for the
public eye; and I trust by the aid of Divine Providence to be able to make
it intelligible and instructive/I thank God for the blessings of Liberty—
the contrast is truly great between freedom and slavery. To be changed
from a chattel to a human being, is no light matter, though the process
with myself practically was very simple. And if I could reach the ears of
every slave to-day, throughout the whole continent of America, I would
teach the same lesson, I would sound it in the ears of every hereditary
bondman, "break your chains and fly for freedom!"

It may be asked why I have written this work, when there has been so
much already written and published of the same character from other
fugitives? And, why publish it after having told it publicly all through
New England and the Western States to multiplied thousands?

My answer is, that in no place have I given orally the detail of my narrative; and some of the most interesting events of my life have never
reached the public ear. Moreover, it was at the request of many friends of
down-trodden humanity, that I have undertaken to write the following
sketch, that light and truth might be spread on the sin and evils of slavery as far as possible. I also wanted to leave my humble testimony on
record against this man-destroying system, to be read by succeeding gen-
erations when my body shall lie mouldering in the dust.

But I would not attempt by any sophistry to misrepresent slavery in
order to prove its dreadful wickedness. For, I presume there are none
who may read this narrative through, whether Christians or slaveholders, males or females, but what will admit it to be a system of the most
high-handed oppression and tyranny that ever was tolerated by an enlightened nation.

HENRY BIBB

NARRATIVE

OF THE

LIFE OF HENRY BIBB.

~~~~~~~~~~~~~~~~~~~~~~

CHAPTER I.

Sketch of my Parentage.—Early separation from my Mother.—
Hard Fare.—First Experiments at running away.—Earnest
longing for Freedom.—Abhorrent nature of Slavery.

I was born May 1815, of a slave mother, in
Shelby County, Kentucky, and was claimed as
the property of David White Esq. He came into possession of my mother long before I was
born. I was brought up in the Counties of Shelby, Henry, Oldham, and Trimble. Or, more correctly speaking, in the above counties, I may safely
say, I was *flogged up;* for where I should have
received moral, mental, and religious instruction,
I received stripes without number, the object of
which was to degrade and keep me in subordina-
tion. I can truly say, that I drank deeply of the
bitter cup of suffering and woe. I have been drag-

ged down to the lowest depths of human degradation and wretchedness, by Slaveholders.

My mother was known by the name of Milldred
Jackson. She is the mother of seven slaves only,
all being sons, of whom I am the eldest. She
was also so fortunate or unfortunate, as to have
some of what is called the slaveholding blood flow-
ing in her veins. I know not how much; but not
enough to prevent her children though fathered by
slaveholders, from being bought and sold in the slave
markets of the South. It is almost impossible for
slaves to give a correct account of their male parentage. All that I know about it is, that my mother
informed me that my fathers name was JAMES BIBB.
He was doubtless one of the present Bibb family of
Kentucky; but I have no personal knowledge of
him at all, for he died before my recollection.

The first time I was separated from my mother, I
was young and small. I knew nothing of my condi
tion then as a slave. I was living with Mr. White
whose wife died and left him a widower with one
little girl, who was said to be the legitimate owner
of my mother, and all her children. This girl was
also my playmate when we were children.

I was taken away from my mother, and hired out
to labor for various persons, eight or ten years in
succession; and all my wages were expended for
the education of Harriet White, my playmate. It
was then my sorrows and sufferings commenced.
It was then I first commenced seeing and feeling
that I was a wretched slave, compelled to work under the lash without wages, and often without

clothes enough to hide my nakedness. I have often
worked without half enough to eat, both late and
early, by day and by night. I have often laid my
wearied limbs down at night to rest upon a dirt
floor, or a bench, without any covering at all, because I had no where else to rest my wearied body,
after having worked hard all the day. I have also
been compelled in early life, to go at the bidding of
a tyrant, through all kinds of weather, hot or cold,
wet or dry, and without shoes frequently, until the
month of December, with my bare feet on the cold
frosty ground, cracked open and bleeding as I walked. Reader, believe me when I say, that no tongue,
nor pen ever has or can express the horrors of
American Slavery. Consequently I despair in finding language to express adequately the deep feeling of my soul, as I contemplate the past history of
my life. But although I have suffered much from
the lash, and for want of food and raiment; I confess that it was no disadvantage to be passed through
the hands of so many families, as the only source
of information that I had to enlighten my mind,
consisted in what I could see and hear from others.
Slaves were not allowed books, pen, ink, nor paper,
to improve their minds. But it seems to me now,
that I was particularly observing, and apt to retain
what came under my observation. But more especially, all that I heard about liberty and freedom to
the slaves, I never forgot. Among other good
trades I learned the art of running away to perfection. I made a regular business of it, and never
gave it up, until I had broken the bands of slavery,

and landed myself safely in Canada, where I was regarded as a man, and not as a thing.

The first time in my life that I ran away, was for
ill treatment, in 1825. I was living with a Mr.
Vires, in the village of Newcastle. His wife was a
very cross woman. She was every day flogging me,
boxing, pulling my ears, and scolding, so that I
dreaded to enter the room where she was. This
first started me to running away from them. I was
often gone several days before I was caught. They
would abuse me for going off, but it did no good.
The next time they flogged me, I was off again; but
after awhile they got sick of their bargain, and returned me back into the hands of my owners. By
this time Mr. White had married his second wife.
She was what I call a tyrant. I lived with her
several months, but she kept me almost half of my
time in the woods, running from under the bloody
lash. While I was at home she kept me all the
time rubbing furniture, washing, scrubbing the
floors; and when I was not doing this, she would
often seat herself in a large rocking chair, with
two pillows about her, and would make me rock
her, and keep off the flies. She was too lazy to
scratch her own head, and would often make me
scratch and comb it for her. She would at other
times lie on her bed, in warm weather, and make
me fan her while she slept, scratch and rub her feet;
but after awhile she got sick of me, and preferred a
maiden servant to do such business. I was then
hired out again; but by this time I had become
much better skilled in running away, and would

make calculation to avoid detection, by taking with me a bridle. If any body should see me in the woods, as they have, and asked "what are you doing here sir ? you are a runaway ?"—I said, "no, sir, I am looking for our old mare;" at other times, "looking for our cows." For such excuses I was let pass. In fact, the only weapon of self defence that I could use successfully, was that of deception. It is useless for a poor helpless slave, to resist a white man in a slaveholding State. Public opinion and the law is against him; and resistance in many cases is death to the slave, while the law declares, that he shall submit or die.

The circumstances in which I was then placed, gave me a longing desire to be free. It kindled a fire of liberty within my breast which has never yet been quenched. This seemed to be a part of my nature ; it was first revealed to me by the inevitable laws of nature's God. I could see that the All-wise Creator, had made man a free, moral, intelligent and accountable being ; capable of knowing good and evil. And I believed then, as I believe now, that every man has a right to wages for his labor; a right to his own wife and children; a right to liberty and the pursuit of happiness; and a right to worship God according to the dictates of his own conscience. But here, in the light of these truths, I was a slave, a prisoner for life; I could possess nothing, nor acquire anything but what must belong to my keeper. No one can imagine my feelings in my reflecting moments, but he who has himself been a slave. Oh ! I have often wept over my con-

dition, while sauntering through the forest, to escape cruel punishment.

"No arm to protect me from tyrants aggression;
No parents to cheer me when laden with grief.
Man may picture the bounds of the rocks and the rivers,
The hills and the valleys, the lakes and the ocean,
But the horrors of slavery, he never can trace."

The term slave to this day sounds with terror to
my soul,—a word too obnoxious to speak—a system
too intolerable to be endured. I know this from
long and sad experience. I now feel as if I had
just been aroused from sleep, and looking back with
quickened perception at the state of torment from
whence I fled. I was there held and claimed as a
slave; as such I was subjected to the will and power of my keeper, in all respects whatsoever. That
the slave is a human being, no one can deny. It is
his lot to be exposed in common with other men,
to the calamities of sickness, death, and the misfor-
tunes incident to life. But unlike other men, he is
denied the consolation of struggling against external diffculties, such as destroy the life, liberty, and
happiness of himself and family. A slave may be
bought and sold in the market like an ox. He is
liable to be sold off to a distant land from his family.
He is bound in chains hand and foot; and his sufferings are aggravated a hundred fold, by the terrible
thought, that he is not allowed to struggle against
misfortune, corporeal punishment, insults and outrages committed upon himself and family; and he
is not allowed to help himself, to resist or escape
the blow, which he sees impending over him.

This idea of utter helplessness, in perpetual bondage, is the more distressing, as there is no period even with the remotest generation when it shall terminate.

"The Sabbath among Slaves."

CHAPTER II

A fruitless effort for education.—The Sabbath among Slaves.—
Degrading amusements.—Why religion is rejected.—Condition of poor white people.—Superstition among slaves.—Education forbidden.

IN 1833, I had some very serious religious impressions, and there was quite a number of slaves in
that neighborhood, who felt very desirous to be
taught to read the Bible.   There was a Miss Davis,
a poor white girl, who offered to teach a Sabbath
School for the slaves, notwithstanding public opinion and the law was opposed to it.   Books were
furnished and she commenced the school ; but the
news soon got to our owners that she was teaching
us to read.   This caused quite an excitement in the
neighborhood.   Patrols* were appointed to go and
break it up the next Sabbath.   They were determined that we should not have a Sabbath School in
operation.   For slaves this was called an incendiary
movement.

The Sabbath is not regarded by a large number
of the slaves as a day of rest.   They have no schools
to go to ; no moral nor religious instruction at all
in many localities where there are hundreds of

---

* Police peculiar to the South.

slaves. Hence they resort to some kind of amusement. Those who make no profession of religion, resort to the woods in large numbers on that day to gamble, fight, get drunk, and break the Sabbath. This is often encouraged by slaveholders. When they wish to have a little sport of that kind, they go among the slaves and give them whiskey, to see them dance, "pat juber," sing and play on the banjo. Then get them to wrestling, fighting, jumping, running foot races, and butting each other like sheep. This is urged on by giving them whiskey; making bets on them; laying chips on one slave's head, and daring another to tip it off with his hand; and if he tipped it off, it would be called an insult, and cause a fight. Before fighting, the parties choose their seconds to stand by them while fighting; a ring or a circle is formed to fight in, and no one is allowed to enter the ring while they are fighting, but their seconds, and the white gentlemen. They are not allowed to fight a duel, nor to use weapons of any kind. The blows are made by kicking, knocking, and butting with their heads; they grab each other by their ears, and jam their heads together like sheep. If they are likely to hurt each other very bad, their masters would rap them with their walking canes, and make them stop. After fighting, they make friends, shake hands, and take a dram together, and there is no more of it.

But this is all principally for want of moral instruction. This is where they have no Sabbath Schools; no one to read the Bible to them; no one to preach the gospel who is competent to expound the Scriptures, except slaveholders. And the slaves, with but few exceptions, have no confidence at all in their preaching, because they preach a pro-slavery doctrine. They say, " Servants be obedient to your masters ;—and he that knoweth his master's will and doeth it not, shall be beaten with many stripes ;— means that God will send them to hell, if they disobey their masters. This kind of preaching has driven thousands into infidelity. They view themselves as suffering unjustly under the lash, without friends, without protection of law or gospel, and the green eyed monster tyranny staring them in the face. They know that they are destined to die in that wretched condition, unless they are delivered by the arm of Omnipotence. And they cannot believe or trust in such a religion, as above named.

The poor and loafering class of whites, are about on a par in point of morals with the slaves at the South. They are generally ignorant, intemperate, licentious, and profane. They associate much with the slaves ; are often found gambling together on the Sabbath ; encouraging slaves to steal from their owners, and sell to them, corn, wheat, sheep, chickens, or any thing of the kind which they can well conceal. For such offences there is no law to reach a slave but lynch law. But if both parties are caught in the act by a white person, the slave is punished with the lash, while the white man is often punished with both lynch and common law. But there is another class of poor white people in the South, who, I think would be glad to see slavery abolished in self defence ; they despise the institution because it is impoverishing and degrading to them and their children.

The slave holders are generally rich, aristocratic, overbearing ; and they look with utter contempt upon a poor laboring man, who earns his bread by the " sweat of his brow," whether he be moral or immoral, honest or dishonest. No matter whether he is white or black; if he performs manual labor for a livelihood, he is looked upon as being inferior to a slaveholder, and but little better off than the slave, who toils without wages under the lash. It is true, that the slaveholder, and non-slaveholder, are living under the same laws in the same State. But the one is rich, the other is poor ; one is educated, the other is uneducated ; one has houses, land and influence, the other has none. This being the case, that class of the non-slaveholders would be glad to see slavery abolished, but they dare not speak it aloud.

There is much superstition among the slaves Many of them believe in what they call " conjuration," tricking, and witchcraft ; and some of them pretend to understand the art, and say that by it they can prevent their masters from exercising their will over their slaves. Such are often applied to by others, to give them power to prevent their masters from flogging them. The remedy is most generally some kind of bitter root ; they are directed to chew it and spit towards their masters when they arc angry with their slaves. At other times they prepare certain kinds of powders, to sprinkle about their masters dwellings. This is all done for the purpose of defending themselves in some peaceable manner, although I am satisfied that there is no virtue at all in it. I have tried it to perfection when I was a slave at the South. I was then a young man, full of life and vigor, and was very fond of visiting our neighbors slaves, but had no time to visit only Sundays, when I could get a permit to go, or after night, when I could slip off without being seen. If it was found out, the next morning I was called up to give an account of myself for going off without permission; and would very often get a flogging for it.

I got myself into a scrape at a certain time, by going off in this way, and I expected to be severely punished for it. I had a strong notion of running off, to escape being flogged, but was advised by a friend to go to one of those conjurers, who could prevent me from being flogged. I went and informed him of the difficulty. He said if I would pay him a small sum, he would prevent my being flogged. After I had paid him, he mixed up some alum, salt and other stuff into a powder, and said I must sprinkle it about my master, if he should offer to strike me ; this would prevent him. He also gave me some kind of bitter root to chew, and spit towards him, which would certainly prevent my being flogged. According to order I used his remedy, and for some cause I was let pass without being flogged that time.

I had then great faith in conjuration and witchcraft I was led to believe that I could do almost as I pleased, without being flogged. So on the next Sabbath my conjuration was fully tested by my going off, and staying away until Monday morning, without permission. When I returned home, my master declared that he would punish me for going off; but I did not believe that he could do it while I had this root and dust; and as he approached me, I commenced talking saucy to him. But he soon convinced me that there was no virtue in them. He became so enraged at me for saucing him, that he grasped a handful of switches and punished me severely, in spite of all my roots and powders.

But there was another old slave in that neighborhood, who professed to understand all about conjuration, and I thought I would try his skill. He told me that the first one was only a quack, and if I would only pay him a certain amount in cash, that he would tell me how to prevent any person from striking me. After I had paid him his charge, he told me to go to the cow-pen after night, and get some fresh cow manure, and mix it with red pepper and white people's hair, all to be put into a pot over the fire, and scorched until it could be ground into snuff. I was then to sprinkle it about my master's bedroom, in his hat and boots, and it would prevent him from ever abusing me in any way. After I got it all ready prepared, the smallest pinch of it scattered over a room, was enough to make a horse sneeze from the strength of it; but it did no good. I tried it to my satisfaction. It was my business to make fires in my master's chamber, night and morning. Whenever I could get a chance, I sprinkled a little of this dust about the linen of the bed, where

they would breathe it on retiring. This was to
act upon them as what is called a kind of love
powder, to change their sentiments of anger, to
those of love, towards me, but this all proved to be
vain imagination. The old man had my money,
and I was treated no better for it.

One night when I went in to make a fire, I avail-
ed myself of the opportunity of sprinkling a very
heavy charge of this powder about my master's bed.
Soon after their going to bed, they began to cough
and sneeze. Being close around the house, watching and listening, to know what the effect would
be, I heard them ask each other what in the world
it could be, that made them cough and sneeze so.
All the while, I was trembling with fear, expecting
every moment I should be called and asked if I
knew any thing about it. After this, for fear they
might find me out in my dangerous experiments
upon them, I had to give them up, for the time
being. I was then convinced that running away
was the most effectual way by which a slave could
escape cruel punishment.

As all the instrumentalities which I as a slave,
could bring to bear upon the system, had utterly
failed to palliate my sufferings, all hope and consolation fled. I must be a slave for life, and suffer
under the lash or die. The influence which this
had only tended to make me more unhappy. I resolved that I would be free if running away could
make me so. I had heard that Canada was a land
of liberty, somewhere in the North; and every wave
of trouble that rolled across my breast, caused me

to think more and more about Canada, and liberty. But more especially after having been flogged, I have fled to the highest hills of the forest, pressing my way to the North for refuge ; but the river Ohio was my limit. To me it was an impassable gulf. I had no rod wherewith to smite the stream, and thereby divide the waters. I had no Moses to go before me and lead the way from bondage to a promised land. Yet I was in a far worse state than Egyptian bondage ; for they had houses and land ; I had none ; they had oxen and sheep ; I had none ; they had a wise counsel, to tell them what to do, and where to go, and even to go with them ; I had none. I was surrounded by opposition on every hand. My friends were few and far between. I have often felt when running away as if I had scarcely a friend on earth.

Sometimes standing on the Ohio River bluff, looking over on a free State, and as far north as my eyes could see, I have eagerly gazed upon the blue sky of the free North, which at times constrained me to cry out from the depths of my soul, Oh! Canada, sweet land of rest—Oh! when shall I get there ? Oh, that I had the wings of a dove, that I might soar away to where there is no slavery; no clanking of chains, no captives, no lacerating of backs, no parting of husbands and wives ; and where man ceases to be the property of his fellow man. These thoughts have revolved in my mind a thousand times. I have stood upon the lofty banks of the river Ohio, gazing upon the splendid steamboats, wafted with all their

magnificence up and down the river, and I thought
of the fishes of the water, the fowls of the air, the
wild beasts of the forest, all appeared to be free, to
go just where they pleased, and I was an unhappy
slave !

But my attention was gradually turned in a
measure from this subject, by being introduced into
the society of young women. This for the time
being took my attention from running away, as
waiting on the girls appeared to be perfectly congenial to my nature. I wanted to be well thought
of by them, and would go to great lengths to gain
their affection. I had been taught by the old superstitious slaves, to believe in conjuration, and it was
hard for me to give up the notion, for all I had been
deceived by them. One of these conjurers, for a
small sum agreed to teach me to make any girl love
me that I wished. After I had paid him, he told me
to get a bull frog, and take a certain bone out of the
frog, dry it, and when I got a chance I must step
up to any girl whom I wished to make love me, and
scratch her somewhere on her naked skin with this
bone, and she would be certain to love me, and
would follow me in spite of herself; no matter who
she might be engaged to, nor who she might be walking with.

So I got me a bone for a certain girl, whom I
knew to be under the influence of another young
man. I happened to meet her in the company of her
lover, one Sunday evening, walking out ; so when I
got a chance, I fetched her a tremendous rasp across
her neck with this bone, which made her jump. But

in place of making her love me, it only madi her angry with me. She felt more like running i.ftei me to retaliate on me for thus abusing her, than she felt like loving me. After I found there was no vir-tue in the bone of a frog, I thought I would try uome other way to carry out my object. I then sought another counsellor among the old superstitious in-fluential siaves ; one who professed to be a great friend of mine, told me to get a lock of hair from the head of any girl, and wear it iu my shoes : this would cause her to love me above all other persons. As there was another girl whose affections I was anxious to gain, but could not succeed, I thought, without trying the experiment of this hair. I slip-ped off one night to see the girl, and asked her for a lock of her hair ; but she refused to give it. Be-lieving that my success depended greatly upon this bunch of hair, I was bent on having a lock before I left that night let it cost what it might. As it was time for me to start home in order to get any sleep that night, I grasped hold of a lock of her hair, which caused her to screech, but I never let go until I had pulled it out. This of course made the girl mad with me, and I accomplished nothing but gained her displeasure.

Such are the superstitious notions of the great masses of southern slaves. It is given to them by tradition, and can never be erased, while the doors of education are bolted and barred against them. But there is a prohibition by law, of mental and religious instruction. The state of Georgia, by an act of 1770, declared " that it shall not be lawful for any number of free negroes, molattoes or mestinos, or even slaves in company with white persons, to meet together for the purpose of mental instruction, either before the rising of the sun or after the going down of the same." 2d Brevard's Digest, 254-5. Similar laws exist in most of the slave States, and patrols are sent out after night and on the Sabbath day to enforce them. They go through their respective towns to prevent slaves from meeting for religious worship or mental instruction.

This is the regulation and law of American Slavery, as sanctioned by the Government of the United States, and without which it could not exist. And almost the whole moral, political, and religious power of the nation are in favor of slavery and aggression, and against liberty and justice. I only judge by their actions, which speak louder than words. Slaveholders are put into the highest offices in the gift of the people in both Church and State, thereby making slaveholding popular and reputable.

CHAPTER III.

My Courtship and Marriage.—Change of owner.—My first born.
—Its sufferings.—My wife abused.—My own anguish.

THE circumstances of my courtship and marriage,
I consider to be among the most remarkable events
of my life while a slave. To think that after I had
determined to carry out the great idea which is so
universally and practically acknowledged among
all the civilized nations of the earth, that I would
be free or die, I suffered myself to be turned aside
by the fascinating charms of a female, who gradually
won my attention from an object so high as that of
liberty ; and an object which I held paramount to
all others.

But when I had arrived at the age of eighteen, which
was in the year of 1833, it was my lot to be introduced to the favor of a mulatto slave girl named
Malinda, who lived in Oldham County, Kentucky,
about four miles from the residence of my owner.
Malinda was a medium sized girl, graceful in her
walk, of an extraordinary make, and active in business. Her skin was of a smooth texture, red
cheeks, with dark and penetrating eyes. She moved in the highest circle* of slaves, and free people of

---

* The distinction among slaves is as marked, as the classes of
society are in any aristocratic community. Some refusing to
associate with others whom they deem beneath them in point of
character, color, condition, or the superior importance of their
respective masters.

color. She was also one of the best singers I ever heard, and was much esteemed by all who knew her, for her benevolence, talent and industry. In fact, I considered Malinda to be equalled by few, and surpassed by none, for the above qualities, all things considered.

It is truly marvellous to see how sudden a man's mind can be changed by the charms and influence of a female. The first two or three visits that I paid this dear girl, I had no intention of courting or marrying her, for I was aware that such a step would greatly obstruct my way to the land of liberty. I only visited Malinda because I liked her company, as a highly interesting girl. But in spite of myself, before I was aware of it, I was deeply in love; and what made this passion so effectual and almost irresistable, I became satisfied that it was reciprocal. There was a union of feeling, and every visit made the impression stronger and stronger. One or two other young men were paying attention to Malinda, at the same time; one of whom her mother was anxious to have her marry. This of course gave me a fair opportunity of testing Malinda's sincerity. I had just about opposition enough to make the subject interesting. That Malinda loved me above all others on earth, no one could deny. I could read it by the warm reception with which the dear girl always met me, and treated me in her mother's house. I could read it by the warm and affectionate shake of the hand, and gentle smile upon her lovely cheek. I could read it by her always giving me the preference of her company; by her pressing invitations to visit even in opposition to her mother's will. I could read it in the language of her bright and sparkling eye, penciled by the unchangable finger of nature, that spake but could not lie. These strong temptations gradually diverted my attention from my actual condition and from liberty, though not entirely.

But oh! that I had only then been enabled to have seen as I do now, or to have read the following slave code, which is but a stereotyped law of American slavery. It would have saved me I think from having to lament that I was a husband and am the father of slaves who are still left to linger out their days in hopeless bondage. The laws of Kentucky, my native State, with Maryland and Virginia, which are said to be the mildest slave States in the Union, noted for their humanity, Christianity and democracy, declare that "Any slave, for rambling in the night, or riding horseback without leave, or running away, may be punished by whipping, cropping and branding in the cheek, or otherwise, not rendering him unfit for labor." "Any slave convicted of petty larceny, murder, or wilfully burning of dwelling houses, may be sentenced to have his right hand cut off; to be hanged in the usual manner, or the head severed from the body, the body divided into four quarters, and head and quarters stuck up in the most public place in the county, where such act was committed.'

At the time I joined my wife in holy wedlock, I was ignorant of these ungodly laws; I knew not that I was propogating victims for this kind of tor ture and cruelty. Malinda's mother was free, and

lived in Bedford, about a quarter of a mile from her
daughter ; and we often met and passed off the time
pleasantly. Agreeable to promise, on one Saturday
evening, I called to see Malinda, at her mother's
residence, with an intention of letting her know my
mind upon the subject of marriage. It was a very
bright moonlight night ; the dear girl was standing
in the door, anxiously waiting my arrival. As I
approached the door she caught my hand with an
affectionate smile, and bid me welcome to her
mother's fireside. After having broached the subject of marriage, I informed her of the difficulties
which I conceived to be in the way of our marriage ;
and that I could never engage myself to marry any
girl only on certain conditions ; near as I can recollect the substance of our conversation upon the
subject, it was, that I was religiously inclined ; that
I intended to try to comply with the requisitions of
the gospel, both theoretically and practically through
life. Also that I was decided on becoming a free
man before I died ; and that I expected to get free
by running away, and going to Canada, under the
British Government. Agreement on those two car-
dinal questions I made my test for marriage.

I said, "I never will give my heart nor hand to
any girl in marriage, until I first know her sentiments upon the all-important subjects of Religion
and Liberty. No matter how well I might love her,
nor how great the sacrifice in carrying out these
God-given principles. And I here pledge myself
from this course never to be shaken while a single
pulsation of my heart shall continue to throb for

Liberty." With this idea Malinda appeared to be well pleased, and with a smile she looked me in the face and said, " I have long entertained the same views, and this has been one of the greatest reasons why I have not felt inclined to enter the married state while a slave; I have always felt a desire to be free ; I have long cherished a hope that I should yet be free, either by purchase or running away. In regard to the subject of Religion, I have always felt that it was a good thing, and something that I would seek for at some future period." After I found that Malinda was right upon these all important questions, and that she truly loved me well enough to make me an affectionate wife, I made proposals for marriage. She very modestly declined answering the question then, considering it to be one of a grave character, and upon which our future destiny greatly depended. And notwithstanding she confessed that I had her entire affections, she must have some time to consider the matter. To this I of course consented, and was to meet her on the next Saturday night to decide the question. But for some cause I failed to come, and the next week she sent for me, and on the Sunday evening following I called on her again ; she welcomed me with all the kindness of an affectionate lover, and seated me by her side. We soon broached the old subject of marriage, and entered upon a conditional contract of matrimony, viz : that we would marry if our minds should not change within one year ; that after marriage we would change our former course and live a pious life ; and that we would embrace the earliest opportunity of running away to Canada for our liberty. Clasping each other by the hand, pledging our sacred honor that we would be true, we called on high heaven to witness the rectitude of our purpose. There was nothing that could be more binding upon us as slaves than this; for marriage among American slaves, is disregarded by the laws of this country. It is counted a mere temporary matter; it is a union which may be continued or broken off, with or without the consent of a slaveholder, whether he is a priest or a libertine.

There is no legal marriage among the slaves of the South; I never saw nor heard of such a thing in my life, and I have been through seven of the slave states. A slave marrying according to law, is a thing unknown in the history of American Slavery. And be it known to the disgrace of our country that every slaveholder, who is the keeper of a number of slaves of both sexes, is also the keeper of a house or houses of ill-fame. Licentious white men, can and do, enter at night or day the lodging places of slaves; break up the bonds of affection in families; destroy all their domestic and social union for life; and the laws of the country afford them no protection. Will any man count, if they can be counted, the churches of Maryland, Kentucky, and Virginia, which have slaves connected with them, living in an open state of adultery, never having been married according to the laws of the State, and yet regular members of these various denominations, but more especially the Baptist and Methodist churches? And

I hazard nothing in saying, that this state of things exists to a very wide extent in the above states.

I am happy to state that many fugitive slaves, who have been enabled by the aid of an over-ruling providence to escape to the free North with those whom they claim as their wives, notwithstanding all their ignorance and superstition, are not at all disposed to live together like brutes, as they have been compelled to do in slaveholding Churches. But as soon as they get free from slavery they go before some anti-slavery clergyman, and have the solemn ceremony of marriage performed according to the laws of the country. And if they profess religion, and have been baptized by a slaveholding minister, they repudiate it after becoming free, and are re-baptized by a man who is worthy of doing it according to the gospel rule.

The time and place of my marriage, I consider one of the most trying of my life. I was opposed by friends and foes; my mother opposed me because she thought I was too young, and marrying she thought would involve me in trouble and difficulty. My mother-in-law opposed me, because she wanted her daughter to marry a slave who belonged to a very rich man living near by, and who was well known to be the son of his master. She thought no doubt that his master or father might chance to set him free before he died, which would enable him to do a better part by her daughter than I could! And there was no prospect then of my ever being free. But his master has neither died nor yet set his son free, who is now about forty years of age, toiling under the lash, waiting and hoping that his master may die and will him to be free.

The young men were opposed to our marriage for the same reason that Paddy opposed a match when the clergyman was about to pronounce the marriage ceremony of a young couple. He said "if there be any present who have any objections to this couple being joined together in holy wedlock, let them speak now, or hold their peace henceforth." At this time Paddy sprang to his feet and said, "Sir, I object to this." Every eye was fixed upon him. "What is your objection?" said the clergyman. "Faith," replied Paddy, "Sir I want her myself."

The man to whom I belonged was opposed, because he feared my taking off from his farm some of the fruits of my own labor for Malinda to eat, in the shape of pigs, chickens, or turkeys, and would count it not robbery. So we formed a resolution, that if we were prevented from joining in wedlock, that we would run away, and strike for Canada, let the consequences be what they might. But we had one consolation; Malinda's master was very much in favor of the match, but entirely upon self fish principles. When I went to ask his permission to marry Malinda, his answer was in the affirmative with but one condition, which I consider to be too vulgar to be written in this book. Our marriage took place one night during the Christmas holydays; at which time we had quite a festival given us. All appeared to be wide awake, and we had quite a jolly time at my wedding party. And notwithstanding our marriage was without license or sanction of law, we believed it to be honorable before God, and the bed undefiled. Our christmas holydays were spent in matrimonial visiting among our friends, while it should have been spent in running away to Canada, for our liberty. But freedom was little thought of by us, for several months after marriage. I often look back to that period even now as one of the most happy seasons of my life; notwithstanding all the contaminating and heart-rending features with which the horrid system of slavery is marked, and must carry with it to its final grave, yet I still look back to that season with sweet remembrance and pleasure, that yet hath power to charm and drive back dull cares which have been accumulated by a thousand painful recollections of slavery. Malinda was to me an affectionate wife. She was with me in the darkest hours of adversity. She was with me in sorrow, and joy, in fasting and feasting, in trial and persecution, in sickness and health, in sunshine and in shade.

Some months after our marriage, the unfeeling master to whom I belonged, sold his farm with the view of moving his slaves to the State of Missouri, regardless of the separation of husbands and wives forever; but for fear of my resuming my old practice of running away, if he should have forced me to leave my wife, by my repeated requests, he was constrained to sell me to his brother, who lived within seven miles of Wm. Gatewood, who then held Malinda as his property. I was permitted to visit her only on Saturday nights, after my work was done, and I had to be at home before sunrise on

Monday mornings or take a flogging. He proved to be so oppressive, and so unreasonable in punishing his victims, that I soon found that I should have to run away in self-defence. But he soon began to take the hint, and sold me to Wm. Gatewood the owner of Malinda. With my new residence I confess that I was much dissatisfied. Not that Gatewood was a more cruel master than my former owner—not that I was opposed to living with Malinda, who was then the centre and object of my affections—but to live where I must be eye witness to her insults, scourgings and abuses, such as are common to be inflicted upon slaves, was more than I could bear. If my wife must be exposed to the insults and licentious passions of wicked slave-drivers and overseers; if she must bear the stripes of the lash laid on by an unmerciful tyrant; if this is to be done with impunity, which is frequently done by slaveholders and their abettors, Heaven forbid that I should be compelled to witness the sight.

Not many months after I took up my residence on Wm. Gatewood's plantation, Malinda made me a father. The dear little daughter was called Mary Frances. She was nurtured and caressed by her mother and father, until she was large enough to creep over the floor after her parents, and climb up by a chair before I felt it to be my duty to leave my family and go into a foreign country for a season. Malinda's business was to labor out in the field the greater part of her time, and there was no one to take care of poor little Frances, while her mother was toiling in the field. She was left at the house to creep under the feet of an unmerciful old mistress, whom.I have known to slap with her hand the face of little Frances, for crying after her mother, until her little face was left black and blue. I recollect that Malinda and myself came from the field one summer's day at noon, and poor little Frances came creeping to her mother smiling, but with large tear drops standing in her dear little eyes, sobbing and trying to tell her mother that she had been abused, but was not able to utter a word. Her little face was bruised black with the whole print of Mrs. Gatewood's hand. This print was plainly to be seen for eight days after it was done. But oh! this darling child was a slave ; born of a slave mother. Who can imagine what could be the feelings of a father and mother, when looking upon their infant child whipped and tortured with impunity, and they placed in a situation where they could afford it no protection. But we were all claimed and held as property ; the father and mother were slaves !

On this same plantation I was compelled to stand and see my wife shamefully scourged and abused by her master ; and the manner in which this was done, was so violently and inhumanly committed upon the person of a female, that I despair in finding decent language to describe the bloody act of cruelty. My happiness or pleasure was then all blasted ; for it was sometimes a pleasure to be with my little family even in slavery. I loved them as my wife and child. Little Frances was a pretty child ; she was quiet, playful, bright, and interesting. She had a keen black eye, and the very image of her mother was stamped upon her cheek ; but I could never look upon the dear child without being filled with sorrow and fearful apprehensions, of being separated by slaveholders, because she was a slave, regarded as property. And unfortunately for me, I am the father of a slave, a word too obnoxious to be spoken by a fugitive slave. It calls fresh to my mind the separation of husband and wife ; of stripping, tying up and flogging ; of tearing children from their parents, and selling them on the auction block. It calls to mind female virtue trampled under foot with impunity. But oh ! when I remember that my daughter, my only child, is still there, destined to share the fate of all these calamities, it is too much to bear. If ever there was any one act of my life while a slave, that I have to lament over it is that of being a father and a husband of slaves. I have the satisfaction of knowing that I am only the father of one slave. She is bone of my bone, and flesh of my flesh ; poor unfortunate child. She was the first and shall be the last slave that ever I will father, for chains and slavery on this earth.

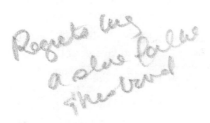

Can a mother forget her suckling child?

The tender mercies of the wicked are cruel.

CHAPTER IV.

My first adventure for liberty.—Parting Scene.—Journey up the river.—Safe arrival in Cincinnati.—Journey to Canada.—Suffering from cold and hunger.—Denied food and shelter by some.—One noble exception.—Subsequent success.—Arrival at Perrysburgh.—I obtained employment through the winter. —My return to Kentucky to get my family.

In the fall or winter of 1837 I formed a resolution that I would escape, if possible, to Canada, for my Liberty. I commenced from that hour making preparations for the dangerous experiment of breaking the chains that bound me as a slave. My preparation for this voyage consisted in the accumulation of a little money, perhaps not exceeding two dollars and fifty cents, and a suit which I had never been seen or known to wear before; this last was to avoid detection.

On the twenty-fifth of December, 1837, my long anticipated time had arrived when I was to put into operation my former resolution, which was to bolt for Liberty or consent to die a Slave. I acted upon the former, although I confess it to be one of the most self-denying acts of my whole life, to take leave of an affectionate wife, who stood before me on my departure, with dear little Frances in her arms, and with tears of sorrow in her eyes as she bid me a long farewell. It required all the moral courage that I was master of to suppress my feelings while taking leave of my little family.

Had Malinda known my intention at that time, it would not have been possible for me to have got away, and I might have this day been a slave. Notwithstanding every inducement was held out to me to run away if I would be free, and the voice of liberty was thundering in my very soul, " Be free oh, man ! be free," I was struggling against a thousand obstacles which had clustered around my mind to bind my wounded spirit still in the dark prison of mental degradation. My strong attachments to friends and relatives, with all the love of home and birth-place which is so natural among the human family, twined about my heart and were hard to break away from. And withal, the fear of being pursued with guns and blood-hounds, and of being killed, or captured and taken to the extreme South, to linger out my days in hopeless bondage on some cotton or sugar plantation, all combined to deter me. But I had counted the cost, and was fully prepared to make the sacrifice. The time for fulfilling my pledge was then at hand. I must forsake friends and neighbors, wife and child, or consent to live and die a slave.

By the permission of my keeper, I started out to work for myself on Christmas. I went to the Ohio River, which was but a short distance from Bedford. My excuse for wanting to go there was to get work. High wages were offered for hands to work in a slaughter-house. But in place of my going to work there, according to promise, when I arrived at the river I managed to find a conveyance to cross over into a free state. I was landed in the village of

Madison, Indiana, where steamboats were landing every day and night, passing up and down the river, which afforded me a good opportunity of getting a boat passage to Cincinnati. My anticipation being worked up to the highest pitch, no sooner was the curtain of night dropped over the village. than I secreted myself where no one could see me, and changed my suit ready for the passage. Soon I heard the welcome sound of a Steamboat coming up the river Ohio, which was soon to waft me beyond the limits of the human slave markets of Kentucky. When the boat had landed at Madison, notwithstanding my strong desire to get off, my heart trembled within me in view of the great danger to which I was exposed in taking passage on board of a Southern Steamboat; hence before I took passage, I kneeled down before the Great I Am, and prayed for his aid and protection, which He bountifully bestowed even beyond my expectation; for I felt myself to be unworthy. I then stept boldly on the deck of this splendid swift-running Steamer, bound for the city of Cincinnati. This being the first voyage that I had ever taken on board of a Steamboat, I was filled with fear and excitement, knowing that I was surrounded by the vilest enemies of God and man, liable to be seized and bound hand and foot, by any white man, and taken back into captivity. But I crowded myself back from the light among the deck passengers, where it would be difficult to distinguish me from a white man. Every time during the night that the mate came round with a light after the hands, I was afraid he would see I was a colored man, and take me up ; hence I kept from the light as much as possible. Some men love darkness rather than light, because their deeds are evil ; but this was not the case with myself; it was to avoid detection in doing right. This was one of the instances of my adventures that my affinity with the Anglo-Saxon race, and even slaveholders, worked well for my escape. But no thanks to them for it. While in their midst they have not only robbed me of my labor and liberty, but they have almost entirely robbed me of my dark complexion. Being so near the color of a slaveholder, they could not, or did not find me out that night among the white passengers. There was one of the deck hands on board called out on his watch, whose hammock was swinging up near by me. I asked him if he would let me lie in it. He said if I would pay him twenty-five cents that I might lie in it until day. I readily paid him the price and got into the hammock. No one could see my face to know whether I was white or colored, while I was in the hammock ; but I never closed my eyes for sleep that night. I had often heard of explosions on board of Steamboats ; and every time the boat landed, and blowed off steam, I was afraid the boilers had bursted and we should all be killed ; but I lived through the night amid the many dangers to which I was exposed. I still maintained my position in the hammock, until the next morning about 8 o'clock, when I heard the passengers saying the boat was near Cincinnati ; and by this time I supposed that the attention of the people would be

3

turned to the city, and I might pass off unnoticed.
There were no questions asked me while on board
the boat. The boat landed about 9 o'clock in the
morning in Cincinnati, and I waited until after
most of the passengers had gone off of the boat; I
then walked as gracefully up street as if I was not
running away, until I had got pretty well up Broadway. My object was to go to Canada, but having
no knowledge of the road, it was necessary for me
to make some inquiry before I left the city. I was
afraid to ask a white person, and I could see no
colored person to ask. But fortunately for me I
found a company of little boys at play in the street,
and through these little boys, by asking them indi-
rect questions, I found the residence of a colored man.

"Boys, can you tell me where that old colored
man lives who saws wood, and works at jobs around
the streets?"

"What is his name?" said one of the boys,

"I forget."

"Is it old Job Dundy?"

"Is Dundy a colored man?"

"Yes, sir."

"That is the very man I am looking for; will
you show me where he lives?"

"Yes," said the little boy, and pointed me out
the house.

Mr. D. invited me in, and I found him to be a true
friend. He asked me if I was a slave from Kentucky,
and if I ever intended to go back into slavery? Not
knowing yet whether he was truly in favor of slaves
running away, I told him that I had just come over to

spend my christmas holydays, and that I was going back. His reply was, " my son, I would never go back if I was in your place ; you have a right to your liberty." I then asked him how I should get my freedom ? He referred me to Canada, over which waved freedom's flag, defended by the British Government, upon whose soil there cannot be the foot print of a slave.

He then commenced telling me of the facilities for my escape to Canada ; of the Abolitionists ; of the Abolition Societies, and of their fidelity to the cause of suffering humanity. This was the first time in my life that ever I had heard of such people being in existence as the Abolitionists. I supposed that they were a different race of people. He conducted me to the house of one of these warm-hearted friends of God and the slave. I found him willing to aid a poor fugitive on his way to Canada, even to the dividing of the last cent, or morsel of bread if necessary.

These kind friends gave me something to eat, and started me on my way to Canada, with a recommendation to a friend on my way. This was the commencement of what was called the under ground rail road to Canada. I walked with bold courage, trusting in the arm of Omnipotence ; guided by the unchangable North Star by night, and inspired by an elevated thought that I was fleeing from a land of slavery and oppression, bidding farewell to hand-cuffs, whips, thumb-screws and chains.

I travelled on until I had arrived at the place

where I was directed to call on an Abolitionist, but I made no stop: so great were my fears of being pursued by the pro-slavery hunting dogs of the South. I prosecuted my journey vigorously for nearly forty-eight hours without food or rest, struggling against external difficulties such as no one can imagine who has never experienced the same: not knowing what moment I might be captured while travelling among strangers, through cold and fear, breasting the north winds, being thinly clad, pelted by the snow storms through the dark hours of the night, and not a house in which I could enter to shelter me from the storm.

The second night from Cincinnati, about midnight, I thought that I should freeze; my shoes were worn through, and my feet were exposed to the bare ground. I approached a house on the road-side, knocked at the door, and asked admission to their fire, but was refused. I went to the next house, and was refused the privilege of their fire-side, to prevent my freezing. This I thought was hard treatment among the human family. But—

"Behind a frowning Providence there was a smiling face,"

which soon shed beams of light upon unworthy me.

The next morning I was still found struggling on my way, faint, hungry, lame, and rest-broken. I could see people taking breakfast from the road-side, but I did not dare to enter their houses to get my breakfast, for neither love nor money. In passing a low cottage, I saw the breakfast table spread with all its bounties, and I could see no male person

"Never mind the money."

CAUGHEY, ENG.

about the house ; the temptation for food was greater than I could resist.

I saw a lady about the table, and I thought that
if she was ever so much disposed to take me up,
that she would have to catch and hold me, and that
would have been impossible. I stepped up to the
door with my hat off, and asked her if she would
be good enough to sell me a sixpence worth of bread
and meat. She cut off a piece and brought it to
me ; I thanked her for it, and handed her the pay,
but instead of receiving it, she burst into tears,
and said "never mind the money," but gently turned away bidding me go on my journey. This was
altogether unexpected to me : I had found a friend
in the time of need among strangers, and nothing
could be more cheering in the day of trouble than
this. When I left that place I started with bolder
courage. The next night I put up at a tavern, and
continued stopping at public houses until my means
were about gone. When I got to the Black Swamp
in the county of Wood, Ohio, I stopped one night
at a hotel, after travelling all day through mud and
snow ; but I soon found that I should not be able to
pay my bill. This was about the time that the
"wild-cat banks" were in a flourishing state, and
"shin plasters"* in abundance ; they would charge
a dollar for one night's lodging.

After I had found out this, I slipped out of the
bar room into the kitchen where the landlady was
getting supper ; as she had quite a number of trav-

---

* Nickname for temporary paper money.

ellers to cook for that night, I told her if she would accept my services, I would assist her in getting supper; that I was a cook. She very readily accepted the offer, and I went to work.

She was very much pleased with my work, and the next morning I helped her to get breakfast. She then wanted to hire me for all winter, but I refused for fear I might be pursued. My excuse to her was that I had a brother living in Detroit, whom I was going to see on some important business, and after I got that business attended to, I would come back and work for them all winter.

When I started the second morning they paid me fifty cents beside my board, with the understanding that I was to return; but I have not gone back yet.

I arrived the next morning in the village of Perrysburgh, where I found quite a settlement of colored people, many of whom were fugitive slaves. I made my case known to them and they sympathized with me. I was a stranger, and they took me in and persuaded me to spend the winter in Perrysburgh, where I could get employment and go to Canada the next spring, in a steamboat which run from Perrysburgh, if I thought it proper so to do.

I got a job of chopping wood during that winter which enabled me to purchase myself a suit, and after paying my board the next spring, I had saved fifteen dollars in cash. My intention was to go back to Kentucky after my wife.

When I got ready to start, which was about the first of May, my friends all persuaded me not to go, but to get some other person to go, for fear I might be caught and sold off from my family into slavery forever. But I could not refrain from going back myself, believing that I could accomplish it better than a stranger.

The money that I had would not pass in the South, and for the purpose of getting it off to a good advantage, I took a steamboat passage to Detroit, Michigan, and there I spent all my money for dry goods, to peddle out on my way back through the State of Ohio. I also purchased myself a pair of false whiskers to put on when I got back to Kentucky, to prevent any one from knowing me after night, should they see me. I then started back after my little family.

CHAPTER V.

I succeeded very well in selling out my goods, and when I arrived in Cincinnati, I called on some of my friends who had aided me on my first escape. They also opposed me in going back only for my own good. But it has ever been characteristic of me to persevere in what I undertake.

I took a Steamboat passage which would bring me to where I should want to land about dark, so as to give me a chance to find my family during the night if possible. The boat landed me at the proper place, and at the proper time accordingly. This landing was about six miles from Bedford, where my mother and wife lived, but with different families. My mother was the cook at a tavern, in Bedford. When I approached the house where mother was living, I remembered where she slept in the kitchen, her bed was near the window.

It was a bright moonlight night, and in looking through the kitchen window, I saw a person lying in bed about where my mother had formerly slept. I rapped on the glass which awakened the person,

in whom I recognised my dear mother, but she
knew me not, as I was dressed in disguise with my
false whiskers on; but she came to the window and
asked who I was and what I wanted. But when I
took off my false whiskers, and spoke to her, she
knew my voice, and quickly sprang to the door,
clasping my hand, exclaiming, " Oh! is this my
son," drawing me into the room, where I was so
fortunate as to find Malinda, and little Frances, my
wife and child, whom I had left to find the fair
climes of liberty, and whom I was then seeking to
rescue from perpetual slavery.

They never expected to see me again in this life.
I am entirely unable to describe what my feelings
were at that time. It was almost like the return
of the prodigal son. There was weeping and rejoicing. They were filled with surprise and fear;
with sadness and joy. The sensation of joy at
that moment flashed like lightning over my afflicted
mind, mingled with a thousand dreadful apprehensions, that none but a heart wounded slave father
and husband like myself can possibly imagine.
After talking the matter over, we decided it was
not best to start with my family that night, as it
was very uncertain whether we should get a boat
passage immediately. And in case of failure, if
Malinda should get back even before daylight the
next morning, it would have excited suspicion
against her, as it was not customary for slaves to
leave home at that stage of the week without permission. Hence we thought it would be the most
effectual way for her to escape, to start on Saturday

night; this being a night on which the slaves of Kentucky are permitted to visit around among their friends, and are often allowed to stay until the afternoon on Sabbath day.

I gave Malinda money to pay her passage on board of a Steamboat to Cincinnati, as it was not safe for me to wait for her until Saturday night; but she was to meet me in Cincinnati, if possible, the next Sunday. Her father was to go with her to the Ohio River on Saturday night, and if a boat passed up during the night she was to get on board at Madison, and come to Cincinnati. If she should fail in getting off that night, she was to try it the next Saturday night. This was the understanding when we separated. This we thought was the best plan for her escape, as there had been so much excitement caused by my running away.

The owners of my wife were very much afraid that she would follow me ; and to prevent her they had told her and other slaves that I had been persuaded off by the Abolitionists, who had promised to set me free, but had sold me off to New Orleans. They told the slaves to beware of the abolitionists, that their object was to decoy off slaves and then sell them off in New Orleans. Some of them believed this, and others believed it not; and the owners of my wife were more watchful over her than they had ever been before as she was unbelieving.

This was in the month of June, 1838. I left Malinda on a bright but lonesome Wednesday night. When I arrived at the river Ohio, I found a small craft chained to a tree, in which I ferried myself across the stream.

I succeeded in getting a Steamboat passage back to Cincinnati, where I put up with one of my abolition friends who knew that I had gone after my family, and who appeared to be much surprised to see me again. I was soon visited by several friends who knew of my having gone back after my family. They wished to know why I had not brought my family with me ; but after they understood the plan, and that my family was expected to be in Cincinnati within a few days, they thought it the best and safest plan for us to take a stage passage out to Lake Erie. But being short of money, I was not able to pay my passage in the stage, even if it would have prevented me from being caught by the slave hunters of Cincinnati, or save me from being taken back into bondage for life.

These friends proposed helping me by subscription; I accepted their kind offer, but in going among friends to solicit aid for me, they happened to get among traitors, and kidnappers, both white and colored men, who made their living by that kind of business. Several persons called on me and made me small donations, and among them two white men came in professing to be my friends. They told me not to be afraid of them, they were abolitionists. They asked me a great many questions. They wanted to know if I needed any help ? and they wanted to know if it could be possible that a man so near white as myself could be a slave ? Could it be possible that men would make slaves of their

own children ? | They expressed great sympathy for
me, and gave me fifty cents each; by this they
gained my confidence.   They asked my master's
name ; where he lived, &c.   After which they left
the room, bidding me God speed.   These traitors,
or land pirates, took passage on board of the first
Steamboat down the river, in search of my owners.
When they found them, they got a reward of three
hundred dollars offered for the re-capture of this
" stray" which they had so long and faithfully been
hunting, by day and by night, by land and by water
with dogs and with guns, but all without success.
This being the last and only chance for dragging me
back into hopeless bondage, time and money was
no object when they saw a prospect of my being re-
taken.

Mr. Gatewood got two of his slaveholding neighbors to go with him to Cincinnati, for the purpose
of swearing to anything which might be necessary
to change me back into property.   They came on
to Cincinnati, and with but little effort they soon
rallied a mob of ruffians who were willing to become
the watch-dogs of slaveholders, for a dram, in connection with a few slavehunting petty constables.

While I was waiting the arrival of my family, I
got a job of digging a cellar for the good lady where
I was stopping, and while I was digging under the
house, all at once I heard a man enter the house;
another stept up to the cellar door to where I was
at work ; he looked in and saw me with my coat off
at work.   He then rapped over the cellar door on
the house side, to notify the one who had entered

the house to look for me that I was in the cellar. This strange conduct soon excited suspicion so strong in me, that I could not stay in the cellar and started to come out, but the man who stood by the door, rapped again on the house side, for the other to come to his aid, and told me to stop. I attempted to pass out by him, and he caught hold of me, and drew a pistol, swearing if I did not stop he would shoot me down. By this time I knew that I was betrayed.

I asked him what crime I had committed that I should be murdered.

" I will let you know, very soon," said he.

By this time there were others coming to his aid, and I could see no way by which I could possibly escape the jaws of that hell upon earth.

All my flattering prospects of enjoying my own fire-side, with my little family, were then blasted and gone ; and I must bid fareweil to friends and freedom forever.

In vain did I look to the infamous laws of the Commonwealth of Ohio, for that protection against violence and outrage, that even the vilest criminal with a white skin might enjoy. But oh ! the dreadful thought, that after all my sacrifice and struggling to rescue my family from the hands of the oppressor ; that I should be dragged back into cruel bondage to suffer the penalty of a tyrant's law, to endure stripes and imprisonment, and to be shut out from all moral as well as intellectual improvement, and linger out almost a living death.

Squire's office.

When I saw a crowd of blood-thirsty, unprincipled slave hunters rushing upon me armed with weapons of death, it was no use for me to undertake to fight my way through against such fearful odds.

But I broke away from the man who stood by with his pistol drawn to shoot me if I should resist, and reached the fence and attempted to jump over it before I was overtaken; but the fence being very high I was caught by my legs before I got over.

I kicked and struggled with all my might to get away, but without success. I kicked a new cloth coat off of his back, while he was holding on to my leg. I kicked another in his eye; but they never let me go until they got more help. By this time, there was a crowd on the out side of the fence with clubs to beat me back. Finally, they succeeded in dragging me from the fence and overpowered me by numbers and choked me almost to death.

These ruffians dragged me through the streets of Cincinnati, to what was called a justice office. But it was more like an office of injustice.

When I entered the room I was introduced to three slaveholders, one of whom was a son of Wm. Gatewood, who claimed me as his property. They pretended to be very glad to see me.

They asked me if I did not want to see my wife and child; but I made no reply to any thing that was said until I was delivered up as a slave. After they were asked a few questions by the court, the old pro-slavery squire very gravely pronounced me to be the property of Mr. Gatewood.

The office being crowded with spectators, many

of whom were colored persons, Mr. G. was afraid to keep me in Cincinnati, two or three hours even, until a steamboat got ready to leave for the South. So they took me across the river, and locked me up in Covington jail, for safe keeping. This was the first time in my life that I had been put into a jail. It was truly distressing to my feelings to be locked up in a cold dungeon for no crime. The jailor not being at home, his wife had to act in his place. After my owners had gone back to Cincinnati, the jailor's wife, in company with another female, came into the jail and talked with me very friendly..

I told them all about my situation, and these ladies said they hoped that I might get away again, and went so far as to tell me if I should be kept in the jail that night, there was a hole under the wall of the jail where a prisoner had got out. It was only filled up with loose dirt, they said, and I might scratch it out and clear myself.

This I thought was a kind word from an unexpected friend : I had power to have taken the key from those ladies, in spite of them, and have cleared myself; but knowing that they would have to suffer perhaps for letting me get away, I thought I would wait until after dark, at which time I should try to make my escape, if they should not take me out before that time. But within two or three hours, they came after me, and conducted me on board of a boat. on which we all took passage down to Louisville. I was not confined in any way, but was well guarded by five men, three of whom were slaveholders, and the two young men from Cincinnati, who had betrayed me.

After the boat had got fairly under way, with these vile men standing around me on the upper deck of the boat, and she under full speed carrying me back into a land of torment, I could see no possible way of escape. Yet, while I was permitted to gaze on the beauties of nature, on free soil, as I passed down the river, things looked to me uncommonly pleasant: The green trees and wild flowers of the forest; the ripening harvest fields waving with the gentle breezes of Heaven; and the honest farmers tilling their soil and living by their own toil. These things seem to light upon my vision with a peculiar charm. I was conscious of what must be my fate; a wretched victim for Slavery without limit; to be sold like an ox, into hopeless bondage, and to be worked under the flesh devouring lash during life, without wages.

This was to me an awful thought; every time the boat run near the shore, I was tempted to leap from the deck down into the water, with a hope of making my escape. Such was then my feeling.

But on a moment's reflection, reason with her warning voice overcame this passion by pointing out the dreadful consequences of one's committing suicide. And this I thought would have a very striking resemblance to the act, and I declined putting into practice this dangerous experiment, though the temptation was great.

These kidnapping gentlemen, seeing that I was much dissatisfied, commenced talking to me, by say-

NARRATIVE OF HENRY BIBB.   67

ing that I must not be cast down; they were going to take me back home to live with my family, if I would promise not to run away again.

To this I agreed, and told them that this was all that I could ask, and more than I had expected.

But they were not satisfied with having recaptured me, because they had lost other slaves and supposed that I knew their whereabouts; and truly I did. They wanted me to tell them; but before telling I wanted them to tell who it was that had betrayed me into their hands. They said that I was betrayed by two colored men in Cincinnati, whose names they were backward in telling, because their business in connection with themselves was to betray and catch fugitive slaves for the reward offered. They undertook to justify the act by saying if they had not betrayed me, that somebody else would, and if I would tell them where they could catch a number of other runaway slaves, they would pay for me and set me free, and would then take me in as one of the Club. They said I would soon make money enough to buy my wife and child out of slavery.

But I replied, " No, gentlemen, I cannot commit or do an act of that kind, even if it were in my power so to do. I know that I am now in the power of a master who can sell me from my family for life, or punish me for the crime of running away, just as he pleases : I know that I am a prisoner for life, and have no way of extricating myself; and I also know that I have been deceived and betrayed by men who professed to be my best friends ; but can all this justify me in becoming a traitor to others ? Can I do that which I complain of others for doing unto me ? Never, I trust, while a single pulsation of my heart continues to beat, can I consent to betray a fellow man like myself back into bondage, who has escaped. Dear as I love my wife and little child, and as much as I should like to enjoy freedom and happiness with them, I am unwilling to bring this about by betraying and destroying the liberty and happiness of others who have never offended me !"

I then asked them again if they would do me the kindness to tell me who it was betrayed me into their hands at Cincinnati ? They agreed to tell me with the understanding that I was to tell where there was living, a family of slaves at the North, who had run away from Mr. King of Kentucky. I should not have agreed to this, but I knew the slaves were in Canada, where it was not possible for them to be captured. After they had told me the names of the persons who betrayed me, and how it was done, then I told them their slaves were in Canada, doing well. The two white men were Constables, who claimed the right of taking up any strange colored person as a slave ; while the two colored kidnappers, under the pretext of being abolitionists, would find out all the fugitives they could, and inform these Constables for which they got a part of the reward, after they had found out where the slaves were from, the name of his master, &c. By the agency of these colored men, they were seized by a band of white ruffians, locked up in jail, and their master sent for. These colored kidnappers, with the Constables, were getting rich by betraying fugitive slaves. This was told to me by one of the Constables, while they were all standing around trying to induce me to engage in the same business for the sake of regaining my own liberty, and that of my wife and child. But my answer even there, under the most trying circumstances, surrounded by the strongest enemies of God and man, was most emphatically in the negative. "Let my punishment be what it may, either with the lash or by selling me away from my friends and home; let my destiny be what you please, I can never engage in this business for the sake of getting free."

They said I should not be sold nor punished with the lash for what I had done, but I should be carried back to Bedford, to live with my wife. Yet when the boat got to where we should have landed, she wafted by without making any stop. I felt awful in view of never seeing my family again; they asked what was the matter? what made me look so cast down? I informed them that I knew I was to be sold in the Louisville slave market, or in New Orleans, and I never expected to see my family again. But they tried to pacify me by promising not to sell me to a slave trader who would take me off to New Orleans; cautioning me at the same time not to let it be known that I had been a runaway. This would very much lessen the value of me in market They would not punish me by putting

irons on my limbs, but would give me a good name,
and sell me to some gentleman in Louisville for a
house servant. They thought I would soon make
money enough to buy myself, and would not part
with me if they could get along without. But I
had cost them so much in advertising and looking
for me, that they were involved by it. In the first
place they paid eight hundred and fifty dollars for
me ; and when I first run away, they paid one hundred
for advertising and looking after me ; and now they
had to pay about forty dollars, expenses travelling
to and from Cincinnati, in addition to the three
hundred dollars reward ; and they were not able to
pay the reward without selling me.

I knew then the only alternative left for me to
extricate myself was to use deception, which is the
most effectual defence a slave can use. I pretended
to be satisfied for the purpose of getting an opportunity of giving them the slip.

But oh, the distress of mind, the lamentable
thought that I should never again see the face nor
hear the gentle voice of my nearest and dearest
friends in this life. I could imagine what must be
my fate from my peculiar situation. To be sold
to the highest bidder, and then wear the chains
of slavery down to the grave. The day star of
liberty which had once cheered and gladdened my
heart in freedom's land, had then hidden itself from
my vision, and the dark and dismal frown of slavery
had obscured the sunshine of freedom from me, as
they supposed for all time to come.

But the understanding between us was, I was not to be tied, chained, nor flogged ; for if they should take me into the city handcuffed and guarded by five men the question might be asked what crime I had committed ?   And if it should be known that I had been a runaway to Canada, it would lessen the value of me at least one hundred dollars.

CHAPTER VI.

Arrival at Louisville, Ky.—Efforts to sell me.—Fortunate escape from the man-stealers in the public street.—I return to Bedford. Ky.—The rescue of my family again attempted.—I start ed alone expecting them to follow.—After waiting some months I resolve to go back again to Kentucky.

WHEN the boat arrived at Louisville, the day being too far spent for them to dispose of me, they had to put up at a Hotel. When we left the boat, they were afraid of my bolting from them in the street, and to prevent this they took hold of my arms, one on each side of me, gallanting me up to the hotel with as much propriety as if I had been a white lady. This was to deceive the people, and prevent my getting away from them.

They called for a bed-room to which I was con ducted and locked within. That night three of them lodged in the same room to guard me. They locked the door and put the key under the head of their bed. I could see no possible way for my escape without jumping out of a high three story house window.

It was almost impossible for me to sleep that night in my peculiar situation. I passed the night in prayer to our Heavenly Father, asking that He would open to me even the smallest chance for escape.

The next morning after they had taken breakfast, four of them left me in the care of Dan Lane. He was what might be called one of the watch dogs of Kentucky. There was nothing too mean for him to do. He never blushed to rob a slave mother of her children, no matter how young or small. He was also celebrated for slave selling, kidnapping, and negro hunting. He was well known in that region by the slaves as well as the slaveholders, to have all the qualifications necessary for his business. He was a drunkard, a gambler, a profligate, and a slave-holder.

While the other four were looking around through the city for a purchaser, Dan was guarding me with his bowie knife and pistols. After a while the others came in with two persons to buy me, but on seeing me they remarked that they thought I would run away, and asked me if I had ever run away. Dan sprang to his feet and answered the question for me, by telling one of the most palpable falsehoods that ever came from the lips of a slaveholder. He declared that I had never run away in my life!

Fortunately for me, Dan, while the others were away, became unwell; and from taking salts, or from some other cause, was compelled to leave his room. Off he started to the horse stable which was located on one of the most public streets of Louis-ville, and of course I had to accompany him. He gallanted me into the stable by the arm, and placed himself back in one of the horses stalls and ordered me to stand by until he was ready to come out.

At this time a thousand thoughts were flashing

through my mind with regard to the propriety of
trying the springs of my heels, which nature had so
well adapted for taking the body out of danger,
even in the most extraordinary emergencies. I
thought in the attempt to get away by running, if I
should not succeed, it could make my condition no
worse, for they could but sell me and this they were
then trying to do. These thoughts impelled me to
keep edging towards the door, though very cautiously. Dan kept looking around after me as if he was
not satisfied at my getting so near to the door. But
the last I saw of him in the stable was just as he
turned his eyes from me; I nerved myself with all
the moral courage I could command and bolted for
the door, perhaps with the fleetness of a much frightened deer, who never looks behind in time of peril.
Dan was left in the stable to make ready for the
race, or jump out into the street half dressed, and
thereby disgrace himself before the public eye.

It would be impossible for me to set forth the
speed with which I run to avoid my adversary; I
succeeded in turning a corner before Dan got sight
of me, and by fast running, turning corners, and
jumping high fences, I was enabled to effect my escape.

In running so swiftly through the public streets, I
thought it would be a safer course to leave the public way, and as quick as thought I spied a high
board fence by the way and attempted to leap over
it. The top board broke and down I came into a
hen-coop which stood by the fence. The dogs bark-
ed, and the hens flew and cackled so, that I feared it

would lead to my detection before I could get out of the yard.

The reader can only imagine how great must have been the excited state of my mind while exposed to such extraordinary peril and danger on every side. In danger of being seized by a savage dog, which sprang at me when I fell into the hen-coop; in danger of being apprehended by the tenants of the lot; in danger of being shot or wounded by any one who might have attempted to stop me, a runaway slave; and in danger on the other hand of being overtaken and getting in conflict with my adversary. With these fearful apprehensions, caution dictated me not to proceed far by day-light in this slaveholding city. At this moment every nerve and muscle of my whole system was in full stretch; and every facility of the mind brought into action striving to save myself from being re-captured. I dared not go to the forest, knowing that I might be tracked by blood-hounds, and overtaken. I was so fortunate as to find a hiding place in the city which seemed to be pointed out by the finger of Providence. After running across lots, turning corners, and shunning my fellow men, as if they were wild ferocious beasts, I found a hiding place in a pile of boards or scantling, where I kept concealed during that day.

No tongue nor pen can describe the dreadful apprehensions under which I labored for the space of ten or twelve hours. My hiding place happened to be between two workshops, where there were men at work within six or eight feet of me. I could imagine that I heard them talking about me, and at other times thought I heard the footsteps of Daniel Lane in close pursuit. But I retained my position there until 9 or 10 o'clock at night, without being discovered ; after which I attempted to find my way out, which was exceedingly difficult. The night being very dark, in a strange city, among slavehold- ers and slave hunters, to me it was like a person entering a wilderness among wolves and vipers, blindfolded. I was compelled from necessity to enter this place for refuge under the most extraor- dinary state of excitement, without regard to its geographical position. I found myself surrounded with a large block of buildings, which comprised a whole square, built up mostly on three sides, so that I could see no way to pass out without expos- ing myself perhaps to the gaze of patrols, or slave catchers.

In wandering around through the dark, I happen- ed to find a calf in a back yard, which was baw- ling after the cow; the cow was also lowing in another direction, as if they were trying to find each other. A thought struck me that there must be an outlet somewhere about, where the cow and calf were trying to meet. I started in the direction where I heard the lowing of the cow, and I found an arch or tunnel extending between two large brick buildings, where I could see nothing of the cow but her eyes, shining like balls of fire through the dark tunnel, between the walls, through which I passed to where she stood. When I entered the streets I found them well lighted up. My heart was gladdened to know there was another chance for my escape. No bird ever let out of a cage felt more like flying, than I felt like running.

Before I left the city, I chanced to find by the way, an old man of color. Supposing him to be a friend, I ventured to make known my situation, and asked him if he would get me a bite to eat. The old man most cheerfully complied with my request. I was then about forty miles from the residence of Wm. Gatewood, where my wife, whom I sought to rescue from slavery, was living. This was also in the direction it was necessary for me to travel in order to get back to the free North. Knowing that the slave catchers would most likely be watching the public highway for me, to avoid them I made my way over the rocky hills, woods and plantations, back to Bedford.

I travelled all that night, guided on my way by the shining stars of heaven alone. The next morning just before the break of day, I came right to a large plantation, about which I secreted myself, until the darkness of the next night began to disappear. The morning larks commenced to chirp and sing merrily—pretty soon I heard the whip crack, and the voice of the ploughman driving in the corn field. About breakfast time, I heard the sound of a horn; saw a number of slaves in the field with a white man, who I supposed to be their overseer. He started to the house before the slaves, which gave me an opportunity to get the attention of one of the slaves, whom I met at the fence, before he started to his breakfast, and made known to him my wants and distresses. I also requested him to bring

me a piece of bread if he could when he came back
to the field.

The hospitable slave complied with my request.
He came back to the field before his fellow laborers,
and brought me something to eat, and as an equivo-
lent for his kindness, I instructed him with regard
to liberty, Canada, the way of escape, and the facilities by the way. He pledged his word that himself and
others would be in Canada, in less than six months
from that day. This closed our interview, and we
separated. I concealed myself in the forest until
about sunset, before I pursued my journey ; and the
second night from Louisville, I arrived again in the
neighborhood of Bedford, where my little family
were held in bondage, whom I so earnestly strove
to rescue.

I concealed myself by the aid of a friend in that
neighborhood, intending again to make my escape
with my family. This confidential friend then carried a message to Malinda, requesting her to meet
me on one side of the village.

We met under the most fearful apprehensions, for
my pursuers had returned from Louisville, with the
lamentable story that I was gone, and yet they were
compelled to pay three hundred dollars to the Cincinnati slave catchers for re-capturing me there.

Daniel Lane's account of my escape from him,
looked so unreasonable to slaveholders, that many
of them charged him with selling me and keeping
the money ; while others believed that I had got
away from him, and was then in the neighborhood,
trying to take off my wife and child, which was true.

Lane declared that in less than five minutes after I run out of the stable in Louisville, he had over twenty men running and looking in every direction after me; but all without success. They could hear nothing of me. They had turned over several tons of hay in a large loft, in search, and I was not to be found there. Dan imputed my escape to my godliness! He said that I must have gone up in a chariot of fire, for I went off by flying; and that he should never again have any thing to do with a praying negro.

Great excitement prevailed in Bedford, and many were out watching for me at the time Malinda was relating to me these facts. The excitement was then so great among the slaveholders—who were anxious to have me re-captured as a means of discouraging other slaves from running away—that time and money were no object while there was the least prospect of their success. I therefore declined making an effort just at that time to escape with my little family. Malinda managed to get me into the house of a friend that night, in the village, where I kept concealed several days seeking an opportunity to escape with Malinda and Frances to Canada.

But for some time Malinda was watched so very closely by white and by colored persons, both day and night, that it was not possible for us to escape together. They well knew that my little family was the only object of attraction that ever had or ever would induce me to come back and risk my liberty over the threshold of slavery—therefore this point was well guarded by the watch dogs of slavery,

and I was compelled again to forsake my wife for a
season, or surrender, which was suicidal to the cause
of freedom, in my judgment.

The next day after my arrival in Bedford, Daniel
Lane came to the very house wherein I was concealed and talked in my hearing to the family about my
escape from him out of the stable in Louisville.
He was near enough for me to have laid my hands
on his head while in that house—and the intimida-
tion which this produced on me was more than I
could bear. I was also aware of the great temptation
of the reward offered to white or colored persons
for my apprehension; I was exposed to other calamities which rendered it altogether unsafe for me to
stay longer under that roof.

One morning about 2 o'clock, I took leave of my
little family and started for Canada. This was almost like tearing off the limbs from my body. When
we were about to separate, Malinda clasped my hand
exclaiming, " oh my soul ! my heart is almost brok-
en at the thought of this dangerous separation.
This may be the last time we shall ever see each
other's faces in this life, which will destroy all my
future prospects of life and happiness forever." At
this time the poor unhappy woman burst into tears
and wept loudly ; and my eyes were not dry. We
separated with the understanding that she was to
wait until the excitement was all over ; after which
she was to meet me at a certain place in the State
of Ohio ; which would not be longer than two months
from that time.

I succeeded that night in getting a steamboat con-

" My heart is almost broken."

veyance back to Cincinnati, or within ten miles of the city. I was apprehensive that there were slave-hunters in Cincinnati, watching the arrival of every boat up the river, expecting to catch me ; and the boat landing to take in wood ten miles below the city, I got off and walked into Cincinnati, to avoid detection.

No my arrival at the house of a friend, I heard that the two young men who betrayed me for the three hundred dollars had returned and were watching for me. One of my friends in whom they had great confidence, called on the traitors, after he had talked with me, and asked them what they had done with me. Their reply was that I had given them the slip, and that they were glad of it, because they believed that I was a good man, and if they could see me on my way to Canada, they would give me money to aid me on my escape. My friend assured them that if they would give any thing to aid me on my way, much or little, if they would put the same into his hands, he would give it to me that night, or return it to them the next morning.

They then wanted to know where I was and whether I was in the city ; but he would not tell them, but one of them gave him one dollar for me, promising that if I was in the city, and he would let him know the next morning, he would give me ten dollars.

But I never waited for the ten dollars. I received one dollar of the amount which they got for be-traying me, and started that night for the north. Their excuse for betraying me, was, that catching runaways was their business, and if they had not done it somebody else would, but since they had got the reward they were glad that I had made my escape.

Having travelled the road several times from Cincinnati to Lake Erie, I travelled through without much fear or difficulty. My friends in Perrysburgh, who knew that I had gone back into the very jaws of slavery after my family, were much surprised at my return, for they had heard that I was re-captured.

After I had waited three months for the arrival of Malinda, and she came not, it caused me to be one of the most unhappy fugitives that ever left the South. I had waited eight or nine months without hearing from my family. I felt it to be my duty, as a husband and father, to make one more effort. I felt as if I could not give them up to be sacrificed on the "bloody altar of slavery." I felt as if love, duty, humanity and justice, required that I should go back, putting my trust in the God of Liberty for success.

CHAPTER VII.

I prepared myself for the journey before named,
and started back in the month of July, 1839.

My intention was, to let no person know my business until I returned back to the North. I went to
Cincinnati, and got a passage down on board of a
boat just as I did the first time, without any misfortune or delay. I called on my mother, and the
raising of a dead body from the grave could not have
been more surprising to any one than my arrival was
to her, on that sad summer's night. She was not
able to suppress her feelings. When I entered the
room, there was but one other person in the house
with my mother, and this was a little slave girl who
was asleep when I entered. The impulsive feeling
which is ever ready to act itself out at the return of
a long absent friend, was more than my bereaved
mother could suppress. And unfortunately for me,
the loud shouts of joy at that late hour of the night,
awakened the little slave girl, who afterwards betrayed me. She kept perfectly still, and never let
either of us know that she was awake, in order that
she might hear our conversation and report it.

Mother informed me where my family was living, and that she would see them the next day, and would make arrangements for us to meet the next night at that house after the people in the village had gone to bed. I then went off and concealed myself during the next day, and according to promise came back the next night about eleven o'clock.

When I got near the house, moving very cautiously, filled with fearful apprehensions, I saw several men walking around the house as if they were looking for some person. I went back and waited about one hour, before I returned, and the number of men had increased. They were still to be seen lurking about this house, with dogs following them. This strange movement frightened me off again, and I never returned until after midnight, at which time I slipped up to the window, and rapped for my mother, who sprang to it and informed me that I was betrayed by the girl who overheard our conversation the night before. She thought that if I could keep out of the way for a few days, the white people would think that this girl was mistaken, or had lied. She had told her old mistress that I was there that night, and had made a plot with my mother to get my wife and child there the next night, and that I was going to take them off to Canada.

I went off to a friend of mine, who rendered me all the aid that one slave could render another, under the circumstances. Thank God he is now free from slavery, and is doing well. He was a messenger for me to my wife and mother, until at the suggestion of my mother, I changed an old friend for a new one, who betrayed me for the sum of five dollars.

We had set the time when we were to start for Canada, which was to be on the next Saturday night. My mother had an old friend whom she thought was true, and she got him to conceal me in a barn, not over two miles from the village. This man brought provisions to me, sent by my mother, and would tell me the news which was in circulation about me, among the citizens. But the poor fellow was not able to withstand the temptation of money.

My owners had about given me up, and thought the report of the slave girl was false; but they had offered a little reward among the slaves for my apprehension. The night before I was betrayed, I met with my mother and wife, and we had set up nearly all night plotting to start on the next Saturday night. I hid myself away in the flax in the barn, and being much rest broken I slept until the next morning about 9 o'clock. Then I was awakened by a mob of blood thirsty slaveholders, who had come armed with all the implements of death, with a determination to reduce me again to a life of slavery, or murder me on the spot.

When I looked up and saw that I was surrounded, they were exclaiming at the top of their voices, " shoot him down! shoot him down!" "If he offers to run, or to resist, kill him!"

I saw it was no use then for me to make any resistance, as I should be murdered. I felt confident that I had been betrayed by a slave, and all my flattering prospects of rescuing my family were gone for ever, and the grim monster slavery with all its horrors was staring me in the face.

I surrendered myself to this hostile mob at once. The first thing done, after they had laid violent hands on me, was to bind my hands behind me with a cord, and rob me of all I possessed.

In searching my pockets, they found my certificate from the Methodist E. Church, which had been given me by my classleader, testifying to my worthiness as a member of that church. And what made the matter look more disgraceful to me, many of this mob were members of the M. E. Church, and they were the persons who took away my church ticket, and then robbed me also of fourteen dollars in cash, a silver watch for which I paid ten dollars, a pocket knife for which I paid seventy-five cents, and a Bible for which I paid sixty-two and one half cents. All this they tyrannically robbed me of, and yet my owner, Wm. Gatewood, was a regular member of the same church to which I belonged.

He then had me taken to a blacksmith's shop, and most wickedly had my limbs bound with heavy irons, and then had my body locked within the cold dungeon walls of the Bedford jail, to be sold to a Southern slave trader.

My heart was filled with grief—my eyes were filled with tears. I could see no way of escape. I could hear no voice of consolation. Slaveholders were coming to the dungeon window in great numbers to ask me questions. Some were rejoicing—some swearing, and others saying that I ought to be hung ; while others were in favor of sending both me and my wife to New Orleans. They supposed that I had informed her all about the facilities for slaves to escape to Canada, and that she would tell other slaves after I was gone; hence we must all be sent off to where we could neither escape ourselves, nor instruct others the way.

In the afternoon of the same day Malinda was permitted to visit the prison wherein I was locked, but was not permitted to enter the door. When she looked through the dungeon grates and saw my sad situation, which was caused by my repeated adventures to rescue her and my little daughter from the grasp of slavery, it was more than she could bear without bursting in tears. She plead for admission into the cold dungeon where I was confined, but without success. With manacled limbs; with wounded spirit; with sympathising tears and with bleeding heart, I intreated Malinda to weep not for me, for it only added to my grief, which was greater than I could bear.

I have often suffered from the sting of the cruel slave driver's lash on my quivering flesh—I have suffered from corporeal punishment in its various forms—I have mingled my sorrows with those that were bereaved by the ungodly soul drivers—and I also know what it is to shed the sympathetic tear at the grave of a departed friend; but all this is but a mere trifle compared with my sufferings from then to the end of six months subsequent.

The second night while I was in jail, two slaves came to the dungeon grates about the dead hour or

night, and called me to the grates to have some conversation about Canada, and the facilities for getting there. They knew that I had travelled over
the road, and they were determined to run away
and go where they could be free. I of course took
great pleasure in giving them directions how and
where to go, and they started in less than a week
from that time and got clear to Canada. I have
seen them both since I came back to the north
myself. They were known by the names of King and
Jack.

The third day I was brought out of the prison to
be carried off with my little family to the Louisville
slave market. My hands were fastened together
with heavy irons, and two men to guard me with
loaded rifles, one of whom led the horse upon which
I rode. My wife and child were set upon another
nag. After we were all ready to start my old master
thought I was not quite safe enough, and ordered
one of the boys to bring him a bed cord from the
store. He then tied my feet together under the
horse, declaring that if I flew off this time, I should
fly off with the horse.

Many tears were shed on that occasion by our
friends and relatives, who saw us dragged off in
irons to be sold in the human flesh market. No
tongue could express the deep anguish of my soul
when I saw the silent tear drops streaming down
the sable cheeks of an aged slave mother, at my departure ; and that too, caused by a black hearted
traitor who was himself a slave :

"I love the man with a feeling soul,
Whose passions are deep and strong;
Whose cords, when touched with a kindred power,
Will vibrate loud and long:

" The man whose word is bond and law—
Who ne'er for gold or power,
Would kiss the hand that would stab the heart
In adversity's trying hour."

"I love the man who delights to help
The panting, struggling poor:
The man that will open his heart,
Nor close against the fugitive at his door.

" Oh give me a heart that will firmly stand,
When the storm of affliction shall lower—
A hand that will never shrink, if grasped,
In misfortune's darkest hour."

As we approached the city of Louisville, we at-
tracted much attention, my being tied and handcuffed, and a person leading the horse upon which I
rode. The horse appeared to be much frightened at
the appearance of things in the city, being young
and skittish. A carriage passing by jammed against
the nag, which caused him to break from the man
who was leading him, and in his fright throw me off
backwards. My hands being confined with irons,
and my feet tied under the horse with a rope, I had
no power to help myself. I fell back off of the horse
and could not extricate myself from this dreadful
condition; the horse kicked with all his might while
I was tied so close to his rump that he could only
strike me with his legs by kicking.

The breath was kicked out of my body, but my
bones were not broken. No one who saw my situation would have given five dollars for me. It was
thought by all that I was dead and would never
come to life again. When the horse was caught the

cords were cut from my limbs, and I was rubbed with whiskey, camphor, &c., which brought me to life again.

Many bystanders expressed sympathy for me in my deplorable condition, and contempt for the tyrant who tied me to the young horse.

I was then driven through the streets of the city with my little family on foot, to jail, wherein I was locked with handcuffs yet on. A physician was then sent for, who doctored me several days before I was well enough to be sold in market.

The jail was one of the most disagreeable places I ever was confined in. It was not only disagreeable on account of the filth and dirt of the most disagreeable kind; but there were bed-bugs, fleas, lice and musquitoes in abundance, to contend with. At night we had to lie down on the floor in this filth. Our food was very scanty, and of the most inferior quality. No gentleman's dog would eat what we were compelled to eat or starve.

I had not been in this prison many days before Madison Garrison, the soul driver, bought me and my family to sell again in the New Orleans slave market. He was buying up slaves to take to New Orleans. So he took me and my little family to the work-house, to be kept under lock and key at work until he had bought up as many as he wished to take off to the South.

The work-house of Louisville was a very large brick building, built on the plan of a jail or State's prison, with many apartments to it, divided off into cells wherein prisoners were locked up after night.

The upper apartments were occupied by females, principally. This prison was enclosed by a high stone wall, upon which stood watchmen with loaded guns to guard the prisoners from breaking out, and on either side there were large iron gates.

When Garrison conducted me with my family to the prison in which we were to be confined until he was ready to take us to New Orleans, I was shocked at the horrid sight of the prisoners on entering the yard. When the large iron gate or door was thrown open to receive us, it was astonishing to see so many whites as well as colored men loaded down with irons, at hard labor, under the supervision of overseers.

Some were sawing stone, some cutting stone, and others breaking stone. The first impression which was made on my mind when I entered this place of punishment, made me think of hell, with all its terrors of torment; such as " weeping, wailing, and gnashing of teeth," which was then the idea that I had of the infernal regions from oral instruction. And I doubt whether there can be a better picture of it drawn, than may be sketched from an American slave prison.

In this prison almost every prisoner had a heavy log chain riveted about his leg. It would indeed be astonishing to a christian man to stand in that prison one half hour and hear and see the contaminating influence of Southern slavery on the body and mind of man—you may there find almost every variety of character to look on. Some singing, some crying, some praying, and others swearing. The people of color who were in there were slaves there without crime, but for safe keeping, while the whites were some of the most abandoned characters living. The keeper took me up to the anvil block and fastened a chain about my leg, which I had to drag after me both day and night during three months. My labor was sawing stone; my food was coarse corn bread and beef shanks and cows heads with pot liquor, and a very scanty allowance of that.

I have often seen the meat spoiled when brought to us, covered with flies and fly blows, and even worms crawling over it, when we were compelled to eat it, or go without any at all. It was all spread out on a long table in separate plates; and at the sound of a bell, every one would take his plate, asking no questions. After hastily eating, we were hurried back to our work, each man dragging a heavy log chain after him to his work.

About a half hour before night they were commanded to stop work, take a bite to eat, and then be locked up in a small cell until the next morning after sunrise. The prisoners were locked in, two together. My bed was a cold stone floor with but little bedding! My visitors were bed-bugs and musquitoes.

CHAPTER VIII.

MOST of the inmates of this prison I have described, were white men who had been sentenced there by the law, for depredations committed by them. There was in that prison, gamblers, drunkards, thieves, robbers, adulterers, and even murderers. There were also in the female department, harlots, pickpockets, and adulteresses. In such company, and under such influences, where there was constant swearing, lying, cheating, and stealing, it was almost impossible for a virtuous person to avoid pollution, or to maintain their virtue. No place or places in this country can be better calculated to inculcate vice of every kind than a Southern work house or house of correction.

After a profligate, thief, or a robber, has learned all that they can out of the prison, they might go in one of those prisons and learn something more— they might properly be called robber colleges; and if slaveholders understood this they would never let their slaves enter them. No man would give much for a slave who had been kept long in one of these prisons.

I have often heard them telling each other how they robbed houses, and persons on the high way, by knocking them down, and would rob them, pick their pockets, and leave them half dead. Others would tell of stealing horses, cattle, sheep, and slaves ; and when they would be sometimes apprehended, by the aid of their friends, they would break jail. But they could most generally find enough to swear them clear of any kind of villany. They seemed to take great delight in telling of their exploits in robbery. There was a regular combination of them who had determined to resist law, wherever they went, to carry out their purposes.

In conversing with myself, they learned that I was notorious for running away, and professed sympathy for me. They thought that I might yet get to Canada, and be free, and suggested a plan by which I might accomplish it ; and one way was, to learn to read and write, so that I might write myself a pass ticket, to go just where I pleased, when I was taken out of the prison ; and they taught me secretly all they could while in the prison.

But there was another plan which they suggested to me to get away from slavery ; that was to break out of the prison and leave my family. I consented to engage in this plot, but not to leave my family.

By my conduct in the prison, after having been there several weeks, I had gained the confidence of the keeper, and the turnkey. So much so, that when I wanted water or anything of the kind, they would open my door and hand it in to me. One of the turnkeys was an old colored man, who swept and cleaned up the cells, supplied the prisoners with water, &c.

On Sundays in the afternoon, the watchmen of the prison were most generally off, and this old slave, whose name was Stephen, had the prisoners to attend to. The white prisoners formed a plot to break out on Sunday in the afternoon, by making me the agent to get the prison keys from old Stephen.

I was to prepare a stone that would weigh about one pound, tie it up in a rag, and keep it in my pocket to strike poor old Stephen with, when he should open my cell door. But this I would not consent to do, without he should undertake to betray me.

I gave old Stephen one shilling to buy me a water melon, which he was to bring to me in the afternoon. All the prisoners were to be ready to strike, just as soon as I opened their doors. When Stephen opened my door to hand me the melon, I was to grasp him by the collar, raise the stone over his head, and say to him, that if he made any alarm that I should knock him down with the stone. But if he would be quiet he should not be hurt. I was then to take all the keys from him, and lock him up in the cell—take a chisel and cut the chain from my own leg, then unlock all the cells below, and let out the other prisoners, who were all to cut off their chains. We were then to go and let out old Stephen, and make him go off with us. We were to form a line and march to the front gate of the prison with a sledge hammer, and break it open, and if we should be discovered, and there shou d be

any out-cry, we were all to run and raise the alarm
of fire, so as to avoid detection. But while we were
all listening for Stephen to open the door with the
melon, he came and reported that he could not get
one, and handed me back the money through the
window. All were disappointed, and nothing done.
I looked upon it as being a fortunate thing for me,
for it was certainly a very dangerous experiment
for a slave, and they could never get me to consent
to be the leader in that matter again.

A few days after, another plot was concocted to
to break prison, but it was betrayed by one of the
party, which resulted in the most cruel punishment
to the prisoners concerned in it ; and I felt thankful
that my name was not connected with it. They
were not only flogged, but they were kept on bread
and water alone, for many days. A few days after
we were put in this prison, Garrison came and took
my wife and child out, I knew not for what purpose,
nor to what place, but after the absence of several
days I supposed that he had sold them. But one
morning, the outside door was thrown open, and
Malinda thrust in by the ruthless hand of Garrison,
whose voice was pouring forth the most bitter oaths
and abusive language that could be dealt out to a
female ; while her heart-rending shrieks and sobbing,
was truly melting to the soul of a father and husband.

The language of Malinda was, " Oh ! my dear
little child is gone ? What shall I do ? my child is
gone." This most distressing sound struck a sympathetic chord through all the prison among the

prisoners. I was not permitted to go to my wife and inquire what had become of little Frances. I never expected to see her again, for I supposed that she was sold.

That night, however, I had a short interview with my much abused wife, who told me the secret. She said that Garrison had taken her to a private house where he kept female slaves for the baset purposes. It was a resort for slave trading profligates and soul drivers, who were interested in the same business.

Soon after she arrived at this place, Garrison gave her to understand what he brought her there for, and made a most disgraceful assault on her virtue, which she promptly repeled; and for which Garrison punished her with the lash, threatening her that if she did not submit that he would sell her child. The next day he made the same attempt, which she resisted, declaring that she would not submit to it; and again he tied her up and flogged her until her garments were stained with blood.

He then sent our child off to another part of the city, and said he meant to sell it, and that she should never see it again. He then drove Malinda before him to the work-house, swearing by his Maker that she should submit to him or die. I have already described her entrance in the prison.

Two days after this he came again and took Malinda out of the prison. It was several weeks before I saw her again, and learned that he had not sold her or the child. At the same time he was buying up other slaves to take to New Orleans. At the expiration of three months he was ready to start with us for the New Orleans slave market, but we never knew when we were to go, until the hour had arrived for our departure.

One Sabbath morning Garrison entered the prison and commanded that our limbs should be made ready for the coffles. They called us up to an anvill block, and the heavy log chains which we had been wearing on our legs during three months, were cut off. I had been in the prison over three months ; but he had other slaves who had not been there so long. The hand-cuffs were then put on to our wrists. We were coupled together two and two—the right hand of one to the left hand of another, and a long chain to connect us together.

The other prisoners appeared to be sorry to see us start off in this way. We marched off to the river Ohio, to take passage on board of the steamboat Water Witch. But this was at a very low time of water, in the fall of 1839. The boat got aground, and did not get off that night ; and Garrison had to watch us all night to keep any from getting away. He also had a very large savage dog, which was trained up to catch runaway slaves.

We were more than six weeks getting to the city of New Orleans, in consequence of low water. We were shifted on to several boats before we arrived at the mouth of the river Ohio. But we got but very little rest at night. As all were chained together night and day, it was impossible to sleep, being annoyed by the bustle and crowd of the passengers on board ; by the terrible thought that we were destined to be sold in market as sheep or oxen ; and

annoyed by the galling chains that cramped our
wearied limbs, on the tedious voyage. But I had
several opportunities to have run away from Garrison before we got to the mouth of the Ohio river.
While they were shifting us from one boat to another
my hands were some times loosed, until they got us
all on board—and I know that I should have broke
away had it not been for the sake of my wife and
child who was with me. I could see no chance to
get them off, and I could not leave them in that condition—and Garrison was not so much afraid of my
running away from him while he held on to my family,
for he knew from the great sacrifices which I had
made to rescue them from slavery, that my attachment was too strong to run off and leave them in his
hands, while there was the least hope of ever getting
them away with me.

CHAPTER IX

Our arrival and examination at Vicksburg.—An account of slave sales.—Cruel punishment with the paddle.—Attempts to sell myself by Garrison's direction.—Amusing interview with a slave buyer.—Deacon Whitfield's examination.—He purchases the family.—Character of the Deacon.

WHEN we arrived at the city of Vicksburg, he intended to sell a portion of his slaves there, and stopped for three weeks trying to sell. But he met with very poor success.

We had there to pass through an examination or inspection by a city officer, whose business it was to inspect slave property that was brought to that market for sale. He examined our backs to see if we had been much scarred by the lash. He examined our limbs, to see whether we were inferior.

As it is hard to tell the ages of slaves, they look in their mouths at their teeth, and prick up the skin on the back of their hands, and if the person is very far advanced in life, when the skin is pricked up, the pucker will stand so many seconds on the back of the hand.

But the most rigorous examinations of slaves by those slave inspectors, is on the mental capacity. they are found to be very intelligent, this is pronounced the most objectionable of all other qualities connected with the life of a slave   In act, it

undermines the whole fabric of his chattelhood ; it
prepares for what slaveholders are pleased to pronounce the unpardonable sin when committed by a
slave. It lays the foundation for running away,
and going to Canada. They also see in it a love
for freedom, patriotism, insurrection, bloodshed, and
exterminating war against American slavery.

Hence they are very careful to inquire whether a
slave who is for sale can read or write. This question has been asked me often by slave traders, and
cotton planters, while I was there for market. After conversing with me, they have sworn by their
Maker, that they would not have me among their
negroes ; and that they saw the devil in my eye ; I
would run away, &c.

I have frequently been asked also, if I had ever
run away ; but Garrison would generally answer
this question for me in the negative. He could
have sold my little family without any trouble, for
the sum of one thousand dollars. But for fear he
might not get me off at so great an advantage, as
the people did not like my appearance, he could do
better by selling us all together. They all wanted
my wife, while but very few wanted me. He asked
for me and my family twenty-five hundred dollars,
but was not able to get us off at that price.

He tried to speculate on my Christian character.
He tried to make it appear that I was so pious and
honest that I would not runaway for ill treatment;
which was a gross mistake, for I never had religion
enough to keep me from running away from slavery
in my life.

But we were taken from Vicksburgh, to the city of New Orleans, were we -were to be sold at any rate. We were taken to a trader's yard or a slave prison on the corner of St. Joseph street. This was a common resort for slave traders, and plant- ers who wanted to buy slaves; and all classes of slaves were kept there for sale, to be sold in pri vate or public—young or old, males or females, chil- dren or parents, husbands or wives.

Every day at 10 o'clock they were exposed for sale. They had to be in trim for showing them- selves to the public for sale. Every one's head had to be combed, and their faces washed, and those who were inclined to look dark and rough, were com- pelled to wash in greasy dish water, in order to make them look slick and lively.

When spectators would come in the yard, the slaves were ordered out to form a line. They were made to stand up straight, and look as sprightly as they could; and when they were asked a question, they had to answer it as promptly as they could, and try to induce the spectators to buy them. If they failed to do this, they were severely paddled after the spectators were gone. The object for using the paddle in the place of a lash was, to con- ceal the marks which would be made by the flogging. And the object for flogging under such circumstances, is to make the slaves anxious to be sold.

The paddle is made of a piece of hickory timber, about one inch thick, three inches in width, and about eighteen inches in length. The part which is applied to the flesh is bored full of quarter inch

auger holes, and every time this is applied to the flesh of the victim, the blood gushes through the holes of the paddle, or a blister makes its appearance. The persons who are thus flogged, are always stripped naked, and their hands tied together. They are then bent over double, their knees are forced between their elbows, and a stick is put through between the elbows and the bend of the legs, in order to hold the victim in that position, while the paddle is applied to those parts of the body which would not be so likely to be seen by those who wanted to buy slaves. (See on page 133.)

I was kept in this prison for several months, and no one would buy me for fear I would run away. One day while I was in this prison, Garrison got mad with my wife, and took her off in one of the rooms, with his paddle in hand, swearing that he would paddle her ; and I could afford her no protection at all, while the strong arm of the law, public opinion and custom, were all against me. I have often heard Garrison say, that he had rather paddle a female, than eat when he was hungry—that it was music for him to hear them scream, and too see their blood run.

After the lapse of several months, he found that he could not dispose of my person to a good advantage, while he kept me in that prison confined among the other slaves. I do not speak with vanity when I say the contrast was so great between myself and ordinary slaves, from the fact that I had enjoyed superior advantages, to which I have already referred. They have their slaves classed off and numbered.

Garrison came to me one day and informed me that I might go out through the city and find myself a master. I was to go to the Hotels, boarding houses, &c.—tell them that my wife was a good cook, wash-woman, &c.,—and that I was a good dining room servant, carriage driver, or porter—and in this way I might find some gentleman who would buy us both; and that this was the only hope of our being sold together.

But before starting me out, he dressed me up in a suit of his old clothes, so as to make me look respectable, and I was so much better dressed than usual that I felt quite gay. He would not allow my wife to go out with me however, for fear we might get away. I was out every day for several weeks, three or four hours in each day, trying to find a new master, but without success.

Many of the old French inhabitants have taken slaves for their wives, in this city, and their own children for their servants. Such commonly are called Creoles. They are better treated than other slaves, and I resembled this class in appearance so much that the French did not want me. Many of them set their mulatto children free, and make slaveholders of them.

At length one day I heard that there was a gentleman in the city from the State of Tennessee, to buy slaves. He had brought down two rafts of lumber for market, and I thought if I could get him to buy me with my family, and take us to Tennessee, from there, I would stand a better opportunity to run away again and get to Canada, than I would from the extreme South.

So I brushed up myself and walked down to the river's bank, where the man was pointed out to me standing on board of his raft, I approached him, and after passing the usual compliments I said :

" Sir, I understand that you wish to purchase a lot of servants and I have called to know if it is o."

He smiled and appeared to be much pleased at my visit on such laudable business, supposing me to be a slave trader. He commenced rubbing his hands together, and replied by saying : " Yes sir, I am glad to see you. It is a part of my business here to buy slaves, and if I could get you to take my lumber in part pay I should like to buy four or five of your slaves at any rate. What kind of slaves have you, sir ?"

After I found that he took me to be a slave trader I knew that it would be of no use for me to tell him that I was myself a slave looking for a master, for he would have doubtless brought up the same objection that others had brought up,—that I was too white ; and that they were afraid that I could read and write ; and would never serve as a slave, but run away. My reply to the question respecting the quality of my slaves was, that I did not think his lumber would suit me—that I must have the cash for my negroes, and turned on my heel and left him !

I returned to the prison and informed my wife of

the fact that I had been taken to be a slaveholder. She thought that in addition to my light complexion my being dressed up in Garrison's old slave trading clothes might have caused the man to think that I was a slave trader, and she was afraid that we should yet be separated if I should not succeed in finding some body to buy us.

Every day to us was a day of trouble, and every night brought new and fearful apprehensions that the golden link which binds together husband and wife might be broken by the heartless tyrant before the light of another day.

Deep has been the anguish of my soul when look- ing over my little family during the silent hours of the night, knowing the great danger of our being sold off at auction the next day and parted forever. That this might not come to pass, many have been the tears and prayers which I have offered up to the God of Israel that we might be preserved.

While waiting here to be disposed of, I heard of one Francis Whitfield, a cotton planter, who want- ed to buy slaves. He was represented to be a very pious soul, being a deacon of a Baptist church. As the regulations, as well as public opinion gener- ally, were against slaves meeting for religious wor ship, I thought it would give me a better opportuni ty to attend to my religious duties should I fall into the hands of this deacon.

So I called on him and tried to show to the best advantage, for the purpose of inducing him to buy me and my family. When I approached him, I felt much pleased at his external appearance—I address-

ed him in the following words as well as I can remember :

"Sir, I understand you are desirous of purchasing slaves ?"

With a very pleasant smile, he replied, "Yes, I
do want to buy some, are you for sale ?"

"Yes sir, with my wife and one child."

Garrison had given me a note to show wherever
I went, that I was for sale, speaking of my wife
and child, giving us a very good character of course
—and I handed him the note.

After reading it over he remarked, "I have a few
questions to ask you, and if you will tell me the
truth like a good boy, perhaps I may buy you with
your family. In the first place, my boy, you are a
little too near white. I want you to tell me now
whether you can read or write ?"

My reply was in the negative.

"Now I want you to tell me whether you have
run away ? Don't tell me no stories now, like a
good fellow, and perhaps I may buy you."

But as I was not under oath to tell him the whole
truth, I only gave him a part of it, by telling him
that I had run away once.

He appeared to be pleased at that, but cautioned
me to tell him the truth, and asked me how long I
stayed away, when I run off ?

I told him that I was gone a month.

He assented to this by a bow of his head, and
making a long grunt saying, "That's right, tell me
the truth like a good boy."

The whole truth was that I had been off in the

state of Ohio, and other free states, and even to Canada; besides this I was notorious for running away, from my boyhood.

I never told him that I had been a runaway longer than one month—neither did I tell him that I had not run away more than once in my life; for these questions he never asked me.

I afterwards found him to be one of the basest hypocrites that I ever saw. He looked like a saint —talked like the best of slave holding Christians, and acted at home like the devil.

When he saw my wife and child, he concluded to buy us. He paid for me twelve hundred dollars, and one thousand for my wife and child. He also bought several other slaves at the same time, and took home with him. His residence was in the parish of Claiborn, fifty miles up from the mouth of Red River.

When we arrived there, we found his slaves poor, ragged, stupid, and half-starved. The food he allowed them per week, was one peck of corn for each grown person, one pound of pork, and sometimes a quart of molasses. This was all that they were allowed, and if they got more they stole it.

He had one of the most cruel overseers to be found in that section of country. He weighed and measured out to them, their week's allowance of food every Sabbath morning. The overseer's horn was sounded two hours before daylight for them in the morning, in order that they should be ready for work before daylight. They were worked from daylight until after dark, without stopping but one half hour to eat or rest, which was at noon.   And at the busy season of the year, they were compelled to work just as hard on the Sabbath, as on any other day.

CHAPTER X.

My first impressions when I arrived on the Deacon's farm, were that he was far more like what the people call the devil, than he was like a deacon. Not many days after my arrival there, I heard the Deacon tell one of the slave girls, that he had bought her for a wife or his boy Stephen, which office he compelled her fully to perform against her will. This he enforced by a threat. At first the poor girl neglected to do this, having no sort of affection for the man—but she was finally forced to it by an application of the driver's lash, as threatened by the Deacon.

The next thing I observed was that he made the slave driver strip his own wife, and flog her for not doing just as her master had ordered. He had a white overseer, and a colored man for a driver, whose business it was to watch and drive the slaves in the field, and do the flogging according to the orders of the overseer.

Next a mulatto girl who waited about the house, on her mistress, displeased her, for which the Deacon stripped and tied her up. He then handed me the lash and ordered me to put it on—but I told

him I never had done the like, and hoped he would
not compel me to do it.   He then informed me that
I was to be his overseer, and that he had bought me
for that purpose.   He was paying a man eight hundred dollars a year to oversee, and he believed I was
competent to do the same business, and if I would
do it up right he would put nothing harder on me
to do ; and if I knew not how to flog a slave, he
would set me an example by which I might be governed.   He then commenced on this poor girl, and
gave her two hundred lashes before he had her
untied.

After giving her fifty lashes, he stopped and lectured her a while, asking her if she thought that
she could obey her mistress, &c.   She promised to
do all in her power to please him and her mistress,
if he would have mercy on her.   But this plea was
all vain.   He commenced on her again ; and this
flogging was carried on in the most inhuman manner
until she had received two hundred stripes on her
naked quivering flesh, tied up and exposed to the

public gaze of all. And this was the example that
I was to copy after.

He then compelled me to wash her back off with
strong salt brine, before she was untied, which was
so revolting to my feelings, that I could not refrain
from shedding tears.

For some cause he never called on me again to
flog a slave. I presume he saw that I was not
savage enough. The above were about the first items
of the Deacon's conduct which struck me with peculiar disgust.

After having enjoyed the blessings of civil and
religious liberty for a season, to be dragged into
that horrible place with my family, to linger out
my existence without the aid of religious societies,
or the light of revelation, was more than I could
endure. I really felt as if I had got into one of the
darkest corners of the earth. I thought I was
almost out of humanity's reach, and should never
again have the pleasure of hearing the gospel sound,
as I could see no way by which I could extricate
myself; yet I never omitted to pray for deliver-
ance. I had faith to believe that the Lord could
see our wrongs and hear our cries.

I was not used quite as bad as the regular field
hands, as the greater part of my time was spent
working about the house; and my wife was the
cook.

This country was full of pine timber, and every
slave had to prepare a light wood torch, over night,
made of pine knots, to meet the overseer with, before daylight in the morning. Each person had to

have his torch lit, and come with it in his hand
to the gin house, before the overseer and driver, so
as to be ready to go to the cotton field by the time
they could see to pick out cotton.   These lights
looked beautiful at a distance.

The object of blowing the horn for them two
hours before day, was, that they should get their bite
to eat, before they went to the field, that they need
not stop to eat but once during the day.   Another
object was, to do up their flogging which had been
omitted over night.   I have often heard the sound
of the slave driver's lash on the backs, of the slaves,
and their heart-rending shrieks, which were enough
to melt the heart of humanity, even among the most
barbarous nations of the earth.

But the Deacon would keep no overseer on his
plantation, who neglected to perform this every
morning.   I have heard him say that he was no
better pleased than when he could hear the overseer's loud complaining voice, long before daylight
in the morning, and the sound of the driver's lash
among the toiling slaves.

This was a very warm climate, abounding with musquitoes, galinippers and other insects which were exceedingly annoying to the poor slaves by night and day, at their quarters and in the field. But more especially to their helpless little children, which they had to carry with them to the cotton fields, where they had to set on the damp ground alone from morning till night, exposed to the scorching rays of the sun, liable to be bitten by poisonous rattle snakes which are plenty in that section of the country, or to be devoured by large alligators, which are often seen creeping through the cotton fields going from swamp to swamp seeking their prey.

The cotton planters generally, never allow a slave mother time to go to the house, or quarter during the day to nurse her child ; hence they have to carry them to the cotton fields and tie them in the shade of a tree, or in clusters of high weeds about in the fields, where they can go to them at noon, when they are allowed to stop work for one half hour. This is the reason why so very few slave children are raised on these cotton plantations, the mothers have no time to take care of them—and they are often found dead in the field and in the quarter for want of the care of their mothers. But I never was eye witness to a case of this kind, but have heard many narrated by my slave brothers and sisters, some of which occurred on the deacon's plantation.

Their plan of getting large quantities of cotton picked is not only to extort it from them by the lash, but hold out an inducement and deceive them by giving small prizes. For example ; the overseer will offer something worth one or two dollars to any slave who will pick out the most cotton in one day ; dividing the hands off in three classes and offering a prize to the one who will pick out the most cotton in each of the classes. By this means they are all interested in trying to get the prize.

After making them try it over several times and weighing what cotton they pick every night, the overseer can tell just how much every hand can pick. He then gives the present to those that pick the most cotton, and then if they do not pick just as much afterward they are flogged.

I have known the slaves to be so much fatigued from labor that they could scarcely get to their lodging places from the field at night. And then they would have to prepare something to eat before they could lie down to rest. Their corn they had to grind on a hand mill for bread stuff, or pound it in a mortar ; and by the time they would get their suppers it would be midnight ; then they would herd down all together and take but two or three hours rest, before the overseer's horn called them up again to prepare for the field.

At the time of sickness among slaves they had but very little attention. The master was to be the judge of their sickness, but never had studied the medical profession. He always pronounced a slave who said he was sick, a liar and a hypocrite ; said there was nothing the matter, and he only wanted to keep from work.

His remedy was most generally strong red pepper tea, boiled till it was red. He would make them drink a pint cup full of it at one dose. If he should not get better very soon after it, the dose was repeated. If that should not accomplish the object for which it was given, or have the desired effect, a pot or kettle was then put over the fire with a large quantity of chimney soot, which was boiled down until it was as strong as the juice of tobacco, and the poor sick slave was compelled to drink a quart of it.

This would operate on the system like salts, or castor oil. But if the slave should not be very ill, he would rather work as long as he could stand up, than to take this dreadful medicine.

If it should be a very valuable slave, sometimes a physician was sent for and something done to save him. But no special aid is afforded the suffering slave even in the last trying hour, when he is called to grapple with the grim monster death. He has no Bible, no family altar, no minister to address to him the consolations of the gospel, before he launches into the spirit world. As to the burial of slaves, but very little more care is taken of their dead bodies than if they were dumb beasts.

My wife was very sick while we were both living with the Deacon. We expected every day would be her last. While she was sick, we lost our second child, and I was compelled to dig my own child's grave and bury it myself without even a box to put it in.

CHAPTER XI.

I attend a prayer meeting.—Punishment therefor threatened.
—I attempt to escape alone.—My return to take my family.
—Our sufferings.—Dreadful attack of wolves.—Our recapture.

SOME months after Malinda had recovered from her sickness, I got permission from the Deacon, on one Sabbath day, to attend a prayer meeting, on a neighboring plantation, with a few old superanuated slaves, although this was contrary to the custom of the country—for slaves were not allowed to assemble for religious worship. Being more numerous than the whites there was fear of rebellion, and the overpowering of their oppressors in order to obtain freedom.

But this gentleman on whose plantation I attended the meeting was not a Deacon nor a professor of religion. He was not afraid of a few old Christian slaves rising up to kill their master because he allowed them to worship God on the Sabbath day.

We had a very good meeting, although our exercises were not conducted in accordance with an enlightened Christianity ; for we had no Bible—no intelligent leader—but a conscience, prompted by our own reason, constrained us to worship God the Creator of all things.

When I returned home from meeting I told the

other slaves what a good time we had at our meet
ing, and requested them to go with me to meeting
there on the next Sabbath. As no slave was allowed
to go from the plantation on a visit without a written pass from his master, on the next Sabbath
several of us went to the Deacon, to get permission
to attend that prayer meeting ; but he refused to let
any go. I thought I would slip off and attend the
meeting and get back before he would miss me, and
would not know that I had been to the meeting.

When I returned home from the meeting as I approached the house I saw Malinda, standing out at
the fence looking in the direction in which I was expected to return. She hailed my approach, not with
joy, but with grief. She was weeping under great
distress of mind, but it was hard for me to extort
from her the reason why she wept. She finally informed me that her master had found out that I had
violated his law, and I should suffer the penalty.
which was five hundred lashes, on my naked back.

I asked her how he knew that I had gone ?

She said I had not long been gone before he called
for me and I was not to be found. He then sent the
overseer on horseback to the place where we were
to meet to see if I was there. But when the overseer got to the place, the meeting was over and I
had gone back home, but had gone a nearer route
through the woods and the overseer happened not
to meet me. He heard that I had been there and
hurried back home before me and told the Deacon,
who ordered him to take me on the next morning,
strip off my clothes, drive down four stakes in the

ground and fasten my limbs to them ; then strike
me five hundred lashes for going to the prayer meeting.   This was what distressed my poor companion.
She thought it was more than I could bear, and that
it would be the death of me.   I concluded then to
run away—but she thought they would catch me
with the blood hounds by their taking my track.
But to avoid them I thought I would ride off on one
of the Deacon's mules.   She thought if I did, they
would sell me.

"No matter, I will try it," said I, "let the consequences be what they may.   The matter can be
no worse than it now is."   So I tackled up the
Deacon's best mule with his saddle, &c., and started that night and went off eight or ten miles from
home.   But I found the mule to be rather trouble-
some, and was like to betray me by braying, especially
when he would see cattle, horses, or any thing of the
kind in the woods.

The second night from home I camped in a cane
break down in the Red river swamp not a great
way off from the road, perhaps not twenty rods, exposed to wild ferocious beasts which were numerous in that section of country.   On that night about
the middle of the night the mule heard the sound
of horses feet on the road, and he commenced stamp-
ing and trying to break away.   As the horses
seemed to come nearer, the mule commenced trying
to bray, and it was all that I could do to prevent
him from making a loud bray there in the woods,
which would have betrayed me.

I supposed that it was the overseer out with the

dogs looking for me, and I found afterwards that I was not mistaken. As soon as the people had passed by, I mounted the mule and took him home to prevent his betraying me. When I got near by home I stripped off the tackling and turned the mule loose. I then slipt up to the cabin wherein my wife laid and found her awake, much distressed about me. She informed me that they were then out looking for me, and that the Deacon was bent on flogging me nearly to death, and then selling me off from my family. This was truly heart-rending to my poor wife; the thought of our being torn apart in a strange land after having been sold away from all her friends and relations, was more than she could bear.

The Deacon had declared that I should not only suffer for the crime of attending a prayer meeting without his permission, and for running away, but for the awful crime of stealing a jackass, which was death by the law when committed by a negro.

But I well knew that I was regarded as property, and so was the ass; and I thought if one piece of property took off another, there could be no law violated in the act; no more sin committed in this than if one jackass had rode off another.

But after consultation with my wife I concluded to take her and my little daughter with me and they would be guilty of the same crime that I was, so far as running away was concerned; and if the Deacon sold one he might sell us all, and perhaps to the same person.

So we started off with our child that night, and

made our way down to the Red river swamps among
the buzzing insects and wild beasts of the forest.
We wandered about in the wilderness for eight or
ten days before we were apprehended, striving to
make our way from slavery; but it was all in vain.
Our food was parched corn, with wild fruit such as
pawpaws, percimmons, grapes, &c. We did at one
time chance to find a sweet potato patch where we
got a few potatoes ; but most of the time, while we
were out, we were lost. We wanted to cross the
Red river but could find no conveyance to cross
in.

I recollect one day of finding a crooked tree
which bent over the river or over one fork of the
river, where it was divided by an island. I should
think that the tree was at least twenty feet from the
surface of the water. I picked up my little child,
and my wife followed me, saying, " if we perish let
us all perish together in the stream." We succeeded
in crossing over. I often look back to that dangerous event even now with astonishment, and wonder
how I could have run such a risk. What would induce me to run the same risk now ? What could
induce me now to leave home and friends and go to
the wild forest and lay out on the cold ground night
after night without covering, and live on parched
corn ?

What would induce me to take my family and go
into the Red river swamps of Louisiana among the
snakes and alligators, with all the liabilities of being
destroyed by them, hunted down with blood hounds,
or lay myself liable to be shot down like the wild

beasts of the forest ?   Nothing I say, nothing but
the strongest love of liberty, humanity, and justice
to myself and family, would induce me to run such
a risk again.

When we crossed over on the tree we supposed
that we had crossed over the main body of the river,
but we had not proceeded far on our journey before
we found that we were on an Island surrounded by
water on either side. We made our bed that night
in a pile of dry leaves which had fallen from off the
trees. We were much rest-broken, wearied from
hunger and travelling through briers, swamps and
cane-brakes—consequently we soon fell asleep after
lying down. About the dead hour of the night I
was aroused by the awful howling of a gang of blood-
thirsty wolves, which had found us out and surrounded us as their prey, there in the dark wilderness many miles from any house or settlement.

My dear little child was so dreadfully alarmed
that she screamed loudly with fear—my wife trembling like a leaf on a tree, at the thought of being
devoured there in the wilderness by ferocious
wolves.

The wolves kept howling, and were near enough
for us to see their glaring eyes, and hear their
chattering teeth. I then thought that the hour of
death for us was at hand ; that we should not live
to see the light of another day ; for there was no
way for our escape. My little family were looking
up to me for protection, but I could afford them
none. And while I was offering up my prayers to
that God who never forsakes those in the hour of

danger who trust in him, I thought of Deacon
Whitfield; I thought of his profession, and doubted
his piety.   I thought of his hand-cuffs, of his whips,
of his chains, of his stocks, of his thumb-screws, of
his slave driver and overseer, and of his religion;
I also thought of his opposition to prayer meetings,
and of his five hundred lashes promised me for attending a prayer meeting.   I thought of God, I
thought of the devil, I thought of hell ; and I thought
of heaven, and wondered whether I should ever see
the Deacon there.   And I calculated that if heaven
was made up of such Deacons, or such persons, it
could not be filled with love to all mankind, and
with glory and eternal happiness, as we know it is
from the truth of the Bible.

The reader may perhaps think me tedious on this
topic, but indeed it is one of so much interest to me,
that I find myself entirely unable to describe what
my own feelings were at that time.   I was so much
excited by the fierce howling of the savage wolves,
and the frightful screams of my little family, that I
thought of the future; I thought of the past; I
thought the time of my departure had come at last.

My impression is, that all these thoughts and
thousands of others, flashed through my mind, while
I was surrounded by those wolves.   But it seemed
to be the will of a merciful providence, that our
lives should be spared, and that we should not be
destroyed by them.

I had no weapon of defence but a long bowie knife
which I had slipped from the Deacon.   It was a
very splendid blade, about two feet in length, and

about two inches in width. This used to be a part of his armor of defence while walking about the plantation among his slaves.

The plan which I took to expel the wolves was a very dangerous one, but it proved effectual. While they were advancing to me, prancing and accumulating in number, apparently of all sizes and grades, who had come to the feast, I thought just at this time, that there was no alternative left but for me to make a charge with my bowie knife. I well knew from the action of the wolves, that if I made no farther resistance, they would soon destroy us, and if I made a break at them, the matter could be no worse. I thought if I must die, I would die striving to protect my little family from destruction, die striving to escape from slavery. My wife took a club in one hand, and her child in the other, while I rushed forth with my bowie knife in hand, to fight off the savage wolves. I made one desperate charge at them, and at the same time making a loud yell at the top of my voice, that caused them to retreat and scatter, which was equivalent to a victory on our part. Our prayers were answered, and our lives spared through the night. We slept no more that night, and the next morning there were no wolves to be seen or heard, and we resolved not to stay on that island another night.

We travelled up and down the river side trying to find a place where we could cross. Finally we found a lot of drift wood clogged together, extending across the stream at a narrow place in the river, upon which we crossed over. But we had not yet surmounted our greatest difficulty. We had to meet one which was far more formidable than the first. Not many days after I had to face the Deacon.

We had been wandering about through the cane brakes, bushes, and briers, for several days, when we heard the yelping of blood hounds, a great way off, but they seemed to come nearer and nearer to us. We thought after awhile that they must be on our track ; we listened attentively at the approach. We knew it was no use for us to undertake to escape from them, and as they drew nigh, we heard the voice of a man hissing on the dogs.

After awhile we saw the hounds coming in full speed on our track, and the soul drivers close after them on horse back, yelling like tigers, as they came in sight. The shrill yelling of the savage blood hounds as they drew nigh made the woods echo.

The first impulse was to run to escape the approaching danger of ferocious dogs, and blood thirsty slave hunters, who were so rapidly approaching me with loaded muskets and bowie knives, with a determination to kill or capture me and my family. I started to run with my little daughter in my arms, but stumbled and fell down and scratched the arm of little Frances with a brier, so that it bled very much ; but the dear child never cried, for she seemed to know the danger to which we were exposed.

But we soon found that it was no use for us to run. The dogs were soon at our heels, and we were compelled to stop, or be torn to pieces by them.

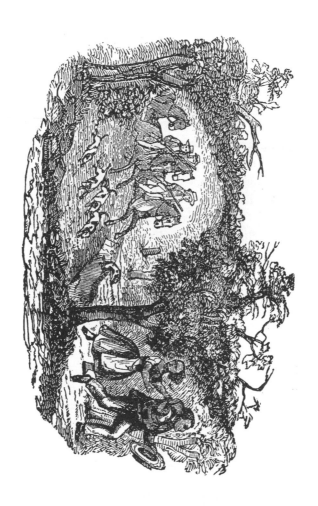

By this time, the soul drivers came charging up on their horses, commanding us to stand still or they would shoot us down.

Of course I surrendered up for the sake of my family. The most abusive terms to be found in the English language were poured forth on us with bitter oaths. They tied my hands behind me, and drove us home before them, to suffer the penalty of a slaveholder's broken law.

As we drew nigh the plantation my heart grew faint. I was aware that we should have to suffer almost death for running off. I was filled with dreadful apprehensions at the thought of meeting a professed follower of Christ, whom I knew to be a hypocrite! No tongue, no pen can ever describe what my feelings were at that time.

CHAPTER XII.

THE reader may perhaps imagine what must have
been my feelings when I found myself surrounded on
the island with my little family, at midnight, by a
gang of savage wolves. This was one of those trying emergencies in my life when there was apparently
but one step between us and the grave. But I had
no cords wrapped about my limbs to prevent my
struggling against the impending danger to which I
was then exposed. I was not denied the consolation of resisting in self defence, as was now the
case. There was no Deacon standing before me,
with a loaded rifle, swearing that I should submit
to the torturing lash, or be shot down like a dumb
beast.

I felt that my chance was by far better among the
howling wolves in the Red river swamp, than before
Deacon Whitfield, on the cotton plantation. I was
brought before him as a criminal before a bar, without counsel, to be tried and condemned by a tyrant's
law. My arms were bound with a cord, my spirit
broken, and my little family standing by weeping.

I was not allowed to plead my own cause, and there was no one to utter a word in my behalf.

He ordered that the field hands should be called together to witness my punishment, that it might serve as a caution to them never to attend a prayer meeting, or runaway as I had, lest they should receive the same punishment.

At the sound of the overseer's horn, all the slaves came forward and witnessed my punishment. My clothing was stripped off and I was compelled to lie down on the ground with my face to the earth Four stakes were driven in the ground, to which my hands and feet were tied. Then the overseer stood over me with the lash and laid it on according to the Deacon's order. Fifty lashes were laid on before stopping. I was then lectured with reference to my going to prayer meeting without his orders, and running away to escape flogging.

While I suffered under this dreadful torture, I prayed, and wept, and implored mercy at the hand of slavery, but found none. After I was marked from my neck to my heels, the Deacon took the gory lash, and said he thought there was a spot on my back yet where he could put in a few more. He wanted to give me something to remember him by, he said.

After I was flogged almost to death in this way, a paddle was brought forward and eight or ten blows given me with it, which was by far worse than the lash. My wounds were then washed with salt brine, after which I was let up. A description of such paddles I have already given in another page. I

was so badly punished that I was not able to work for several days. After being flogged as described, they took me off several miles to a shop and had a heavy iron collar riveted on my neck with prongs extending above my head, on the end of which there was a small bell. I was not able to reach the bell with my hand. This heavy load of iron I was compelled to wear for six weeks. I never was allowed to lie in the same house with my family again while I was the slave of Whitfield. I either had to sleep with my feet in the stocks, or be chained with a large log chain to a log over night, with no bed or bedding to rest my wearied limbs on, after toiling all day in the cotton field. I suffered almost death while kept in this confinement ; and he had ordered the overseer never to let me loose again; saying that I thought of getting free by running off, but no negro should ever get away from him alive.

I have omitted to state that this was the second time I had run away from him ; while I was gone the first time, he extorted from my wife the fact that I had been in the habit of running away, before we left Kentucky ; that I had been to Canada, and that I was trying to learn the art of reading and writing. All this was against me.

It is true that I was striving to learn myself to write. I was a kind of a house servant and was frequently sent off on errands, but never without a written pass ; and on Sundays I have sometimes got permission to visit our neighbor's slaves, and I have often tried to write myself a pass.

Whenever I got hold of an old letter that had

been thrown away, or a piece of white paper, I would save it to write on. I have often gone off in the woods and spent the greater part of the day alone, trying to learn to write myself a pass, by writing on the backs of old letters; copying after the pass that had been written by Whitfield; by so doing I got the use of the pen and could form letters as well as I can now, but knew not what they were.

The Deacon had an old slave by the name of Jack whom he bought about the time that he bought me. Jack was born in the State of Virginia. He had some idea of freedom; had often run away, but was very ignorant; knew not where to go for refuge; but understood all about providing something to eat when unjustly deprived of it.

So for ill treatment, we concluded to take a tramp together. I was to be the pilot, while Jack was to carry the baggage and keep us in provisions. Before we started, I managed to get hold of a suit of clothes the Deacon possessed, with his gun, ammunition and bowie knife. We also procured a blanket, a joint of meat, and some bread.

We started in a northern direction, being bound for the city of Little Rock, State of Arkansas. We travelled by night and laid by in the day, being guided by the unchangeable North Star; but at length, our provisions gave out, and it was Jack's place to get more. We came in sight of a large plantation one morning, where we saw people of color, and Jack said he could get something there, among the slaves, that night, for us to eat. So we concealed ourselves, in sight of this plantation until about bed time, when we saw the lights extinguished.

During the day we saw a female slave passing from the dwelling house to the kitchen as if she was the cook; the house being about three rods from the landlord's dwelling. After we supposed the whites were all asleep, Jack slipped up softly to the kitchen to try his luck with the cook, to see if he could get any thing from her to eat.

I would remark that the domestic slaves are often found to be traitors to their own people, for the purpose of gaining favor with their masters; and they are encouraged and trained up by them to report every plot they know of being formed about stealing any thing, or running away, or any thing of the kind; and for which they are paid. This is one of the principal causes of the slaves being divided among themselves, and without which they could not be held in bondage one year, and perhaps not half that time.

I now proceed to describe the unsuccessful attempt of poor Jack to obtain something from the female slave to satisfy hunger. The planter's house was situated on an elevated spot on the side of a hill. The fencing about the house and garden was very crookedly laid up with rails. The night was rather dark and rainy, and Jack left me with the understanding that I was to stay at a certain place until he returned. I cautioned him before he left me to be very careful—and after he started, I left the place where he was to find me when he returned, for fear something might happen which might lead to my detection, should I remain at that spot. So I left it and went off where I could see the house, and that place too.

Jack had not long been gone, before I heard a great noise ; a man, crying out with a loud voice, " Catch him! Catch him !" and hissing the dogs on, and they were close after Jack. The next thing I saw, was Jack running for life, and an old white man after him, with a gun, and his dogs. The fence being on sidling ground, and wet with the rain, when Jack run against it he knocked down several pannels of it and fell, tumbling over and over to the foot of the hill ; but soon recovered and ran to where he had left me ; but I was gone. The dogs were still after him.

There happened to be quite a thicket of small oak shrubs and bushes in the direction he ran. I think he might have been heard running and straddling bushes a quarter of a mile ! The poor fellow hurt himself considerably in straddling over bushes in that way, in making his escape.

Finally the dogs relaxed their chase and poor Jack and myself again met in the thick forest. He said when he rapped on the cook-house door, the colored woman came to the door. He asked her if she would let him have a bite of bread if she had it, that he was a poor hungry absconding slave. But she made no reply to what he said but immediately sounded the alarm by calling loudly after her master, saying, " here is a runaway negro !" Jack said that he was going to knock her down but her master was out within one moment, and he had to run for his life.

As soon as we got our eyes fixed on the North Star again, we started on our way. We travelled on a few miles and came to another large plantation, where Jack was determined to get something to eat. He left me at a certain place while he went up to the house to find something if possible.

He was gone some time before he returned, but when I saw him coming, he appeared to be very heavy loaded with a bag of something. We walked off pretty fast until we got some distance in the woods. Jack then stopped and opened his bag in which he had six small pigs. I asked him how he got them without making any noise ; and he said that he found a bed of hogs, in which there were the pigs with their mother. While the pigs were sucking he crawled up to them without being discovered by the sow, and took them by their necks one after another, and choked them to death, and slipped them into his bag !

We intended to travel on all that night and lay by the next day in the forest and cook up our pigs. We fell into a large road leading on the direction which we were travelling, and had not proceeded over three miles before I found a white hat lying in the road before me. Jack being a little behind me I stopped until he came up, and showed it to him. He picked it up. We looked a few steps farther and saw a man lying by the way, either asleep or intoxicated, as we supposed.

I told Jack not to take the hat, but he would not

obey me. He had only a piece of a hat himself, which he left in exchange for the other. We travelled on about five miles farther, and in passing a house discovered a large turkey sitting on the fence, which temptation was greater than Jack could resist. Notwithstanding he had six very nice fat little pigs on his back, he stepped up and took the turkey off the fence.

By this time it was getting near day-light and we left the road and went off a mile or so among the hills of the forest, where we struck camp for the day. We then picked our turkey, dressed our pigs, and cooked two of them. We got the hair off by singeing them over the fire, and after we had eaten all we wanted, one of us slept while the other watched. We had flint, punk, and powder to strike fire with. A little after dark the next night, we started on our way.

But about ten o'clock that night just as we were passing through a thick skirt of woods, five men sprang out before us with fire-arms, swearing if we moved another step, they would shoot us down; and each man having his gun drawn up for shooting we had no chance to make any defence, and surren dered sooner than run the risk of being killed.

They had been lying in wait for us there, for several hours. They had seen a reward out, for notices were put up in the most public places, that fifty dollars would be paid for me, dead or alive, if I should not return home within so many days. And the reader will remember that neither Jack nor myself was able to read the advertisement. It was of very little consequence with the slave catchers, whether they killed us or took us alive, for the reward was the same to them.

After we were taken and tied, one of the men declared to me that he would have shot me dead just as sure as he lived, if I had moved one step after they commanded us to stop. He had his gun levelled at my breast, already cocked, and his finger on the trigger. The way they came to find us out was from the circumstance of Jack's taking the man's hat in connection with the advertisement. The man whose hat was taken was drunk; and the next morning when he came to look for his hat it was gone and Jack's old hat lying in the place of it; and in looking round he saw the tracks of two persons in the dust, who had passed during the night, and one of them having but three toes on one foot. He followed these tracks until they came to a large mud pond, in a lane on one side of which a person might pass dry shod; but the man with three toes on one foot had plunged through the mud. This led the man to think there must be runaway slaves, and from out of that neighborhood; for all persons in that settlement knew which side of that mud hole to go. He then got others to go with him, and they followed us until our track left the road. They supposed that we had gone off in the woods to lay by until night, after which we should pursue our course.

After we were captured they took us off several miles to where one of them lived, and kept us over night. One of our pigs was cooked for us to eat that night ; and the turkey the next morning. But we were both tied that night with our hands behind us, and our feet were also tied. The doors were locked, and a bedstead was set against the front door, and two men slept in it to prevent our getting out in the night. They said that they knew how to catch runaway negroes, and how to keep them after they were caught.

They remarked that after they found we had stopped to lay by until night, and they saw from our tracks what direction we were travelling, they went about ten miles on that direction, and hid by the road side until we came up that night. That night after all had got fast to sleep, I thought I would try to get out, and I should have succeeded, if I could have moved the bed from the door. I managed to untie myself and crawled under the bed which was placed at the door, and strove to remove it, but in so doing I awakened the men and they got up and confined me again, and watched me until day light, each with a gun in hand.

The next morning they started with us back to

Deacon Whitfield's plantation; but when they got
within ten miles of where he lived they stopped at
a public house to stay over night; and who should
we meet there but the Deacon, who was then out
looking for me.

The reader may well imagine how I felt to meet
him. I had almost as soon come in contact with
Satan himself. He had two long poles or sticks of
wood brought in to confine us to. I was compelled
to lie on my back across one of those sticks with
my arms out, and have them lashed fast to the log
with a cord. My feet were also tied to the other,
and there I had to lie all that night with my back
across this stick of wood, and my feet and hands
tied. I suffered that night under the most excru-
ciating pain. From the tight binding of the cord
the circulation of the blood in my arms and feet
was almost entirely stopped. If the night had been
much longer I must have died in that confinement.

The next morning we were taken back to the
Deacon's farm, and both flogged for going off, and
set to work. But there was some allowance made
for me on account of my being young. They said
that they knew old Jack had pursuaded me off, or I
never would have gone. And the Deacon's wife
begged that I might be favored some, for that time,
as Jack had influenced me, so as to bring up my old
habits of running away that I had entirely given up.

CHAPTER XIII.

I am sold to gamblers.——They try to purchase my family.—
Our parting scene.—My good usage.—I am sold to an Indian.
—His confidence in my integrity manifested.

THE reader will remember that this brings me
back to the time the Deacon had ordered me to
be kept in confinement until he got a chance to sell
me, and that no negro should ever get away from
him and live. Some days after this we were all out
at the gin house ginning cotton, which was situated
on the road side, and there came along a company
of men, fifteen or twenty in number, who were
Southern sportsmen. Their attention was attract-
ed by the load of iron which was fastened about my
neck with a bell attached. They stopped and asked
the Deacon what that bell was put on my neck for ?
and he said it was to keep me from running away, &c.

They remarked that I looked as if I might be
a smart negro, and asked if he wanted to sell me.
The reply was, yes. They then got off their horses
and struck a bargain with him for me. They bought
me at a reduced price for speculation.

After they had purchased me, I asked the privilege of going to the house to take leave of my family
before I left, which was granted by the sportsmen.
But the Deacon said I should never again step my

foot inside of his yard; and advised the sportsmen not to take the irons from my neck until they had sold me; that if they gave me the least chance I would run away from them, as I did from him. So I was compelled to mount a horse and go off with them as I supposed, never again to meet my family in this life.

We had not proceeded far before they informed me that they had bought me to sell again, and if they kept the irons on me it would be detrimental to the sale, and that they would therefore take off the irons and dress me up like a man, and throw away the old rubbish which I then had on; and they would sell me to some one who would treat me better than Deacon Whitfield. After they had cut off the irons and dressed me up, they crossed over Red River into Texas, where they spent some time horse racing and gambling; and although they were wick-ed black legs of the basest character, it is but due to them to say, that they used me far better than ever the Deacon did. They gave me plenty to eat and put nothing hard on me to do. They expressed much sympathy for me in my bereavement; and almost every day they gave me money more or less, and by my activity in waiting on them, and upright conduct, I got into the good graces of them all, but they could not get any person to buy me on account of the amount of intelligence which they supposed me to have; for many of them thought that I could read and write. When they left Texas, they intend-ed to go to the Indian Territory west of the Missis-sippi, to attend a great horse race which was to

take place.   Not being much out of their way to go
past Deacon Whitfield's again, I prevailed on them
to call on him for the purpose of trying to purchase
my wife and child; and I promised them that if they
would buy my wife and child, I would get some person to purchase us from them.   So they tried to
grant my request by calling on the Deacon, and
trying to make the purchase.   As we approached
the Deacon's plantation, my heart was filled with a
thousand painful and fearful apprehensions.   I had
the fullest confidence in the blacklegs with whom I
travelled, believing that they would do according
to promise, and go to the fullest extent of their
ability to restore peace and consolation to a bereaved family—to re-unite husband and wife, parent and
child, who had long been severed by slavery through
the agency of Deacon Whitfield.   But I knew his
determination in relation to myself, and I feared his
wicked opposition to a restoration of myself and
little family, which he had divided, and soon found
that my fears were not without foundation.

When we rode up and walked into his yard, the
Deacon came out and spoke to all but myself; and
not finding me in tattered rags as a substitute for
clothes, nor having an iron collar or bell about my
neck, as was the case when he sold me, he appeared to
be much displeased.

" What did you bring that negro back here for ?"
said he.

" We have come to try to buy his wife and child ;
for we can find no one who is willing to buy him
6

alone; and we will either buy or sell so that the family may be together," said they.

While this conversation was going on, my poor bereaved wife, who never expected to see me again in this life, spied me and came rushing to me through the crowd, throwing her arms about my neck exclaiming in the most sympathetic tones, " Oh ! my dear husband ! I never expected to see you again !" The poor woman was bathed with tears of sorrow and grief. But no sooner had she reached me, than the Deacon peremptorily commanded her to go to her work. This she did not obey, but prayed that her master would not separate us again, as she was there alone, far from friends and relations whom she should never meet again And now to take away her husband, her last and only true friend, would be like taking her life !

But such appeals made no impression on the unfeeling Deacon's heart. While he was storming with abusive language, and even using the gory lash with hellish vengeance to separate husband and wife, I could see the sympathetic tear-drop, stealing its way down the cheek of the profligate and black-leg, whose object it now was to bind up the broken heart of a wife, and restore to the arms of a bereaved husband, his companion.

They were disgusted at the conduct of Whitfield and cried out shame, even in his presence. They told him that they would give a thousand dollars for my wife and child, or any thing in reason. But no ! he would sooner see me to the devil than indulge or gratify me after my having run away from him; and if they did not remove me from his presence very soon, he said he should make them suffer for it.

But all this, and even the gory lash had yet failed to break the grasp of poor Malinda, whose prospect of connubial, social, and future happiness was all at stake. When the dear woman saw there was no help for us, and that we should soon be separated forever, in the name of Deacon Whitfield, and American slavery to meet no more as husband and wife, parent and child--the last and loudest appeal was made on our knees. We appealed to the God of justice and to the sacred ties of humanity; but this was all in vain. The louder we prayed the harder he whipped, amid the most heart-rending shrieks from the poor slave mother and child, as little Frances stood by, sobbing at the abuse inflicted on her mother.

"Oh! how shall I give my husband the parting hand never to meet again ? This will surely break my heart," were her parting words.

I can never describe to the reader the awful reality of that separation—for it was enough to chill the blood and stir up the deepest feeling of revenge in the hearts of slaveholding black-legs, who as they stood by, were threatening, some weeping, some swearing and others declaring vengeance against such treatment being inflicted on a human being. As we left the plantation, as far as we could see and hear, the Deacon was still laying on the gory lash, trying to prevent poor Malinda from weeping over the loss of her departed husband, who was then, by the hellish laws of slavery, to her, theoretically and

"Oh! how shall I give my husband the parting
hand never to meet again."

practically dead. One of the black-legs exclaimed that hell was full of just such Deacon's as Whitfield. This occurred in December, 1840. I have never seen Malinda, since that period. I never expect to see her again.

The sportsmen to whom I was sold, showed their sympathy for me not only by word but by deeds. They said that they had made the most liberal offer to Whitfield, to buy or sell for the sole purpose of reuniting husband and wife. But he stood out against it—they felt sorry for me. They said they had bought me to speculate on, and were not able to lose what they had paid for me. But they would make a bargain with me, if I was willing, and would lay a plan, by which I might yet get free. If I would use my influence so as to get some person to buy me while traveling about with them, they would give me a portion of the money for which they sold me, and they would also give me directions by which I might yet run away and go to Canada.

This offer I accepted, and the plot was made. They advised me to act very stupid in language and thought, but in business I must be spry ; and that I must persuade men to buy me, and promise them that I would be smart.

We passed through the State of Arkansas and stopped at many places, horse-racing and gambling. My business was to drive a wagon in which they carried their gambling apparatus, clothing, &c. I had also to black boots and attend to horses. We stopped at Fayettville, where they almost lost me, betting on a horse race.

They went from thence to the Indian Territory among the Cherokee Indians, to attend the great races which were to take place there. During the races there was a very wealthy half Indian of that tribe, who became much attached to me, and had some notion of buying me, after hearing that I was for sale, being a slaveholder. The idea struck me rather favorable, for several reasons. First, I thought I should stand a better chance to get away from an Indian than from a white man. Second, he wanted me only for a kind of a body servant to wait on him—and in this case I knew that I should fare better than I should in the field. And my owners also told me that it would be an easy place to get away from. I took their advice for fear I might not get another chance so good as that, and prevailed on the man to buy me. He paid them nine hundred dollars, in gold and silver, for me. I saw the money counted out.

After the purchase was made, the sportsmen got me off to one side, and according to promise they gave me a part of the money, and directions how to get from there to Canada. They also advised me how to act until I got a good chance to run away. I was to embrace the earliest opportunity of getting away, before they should become acquainted with me. I was never to let it be known where I was from, nor where I was born. I was to act quite stupid and ignorant. And when I started I was to go up the boundary line, between the Indian Territory and the States of Arkansas and Missouri, and this would fetch me out on the Missouri river, near

Jefferson city, the capital of Missouri. I was to travel at first by night, aud to lay by in day light, until I got out of danger.

The same afternoon that the Indian bought me, he started with me to his residence, which was fifty or sixty miles distant. And so great was his confidence in me, that he intrusted me to carry his money. The amount must have been at least five hundred dollars, which was all in gold and silver; and when we stopped over night the money and horses were all left in my charge.

It would have been a very easy matter for me to have taken one of the best horses, with the money, and run off. And the temptation was truly great to a man like myself, who was watching for the earliest opportunity to escape ; and I felt confident that I should never have a better opportunity to escape full handed than then,

CHAPTER XIV.

Character of my Indian Master.—Slavery among the Indians less cruel.—Indian carousal.—Enfeebled health of my Indian Master.—His death.—My escape.—Adventure in a wigwam.—Successful progress toward liberty.

THE next morning I went home with my new master; and by the way it is only doing justice to the dead to say, that he was the most reasonable, and humane slaveholder that I have ever belonged to. He was the last man that pretended to claim property in my person; and although I have freely given the names and residences of all others who have held me as a slave, for prudential reasons I shall omit giving the name of this individual.

He was the owner of a large plantation and quite a number of slaves. He raised corn and wheat for his own consumption only. There was no cotton, tobacco, or anything of the kind produced among them for market. And I found this difference between negro slavery among the Indians, and the same thing among the white slaveholders of the South. The Indians allow their slaves enough to eat and wear. They have no overseers to whip nor drive them. If a slave offends his master, he sometimes, in a heat of passion, undertakes to chastise him; but it is as often the case as otherwise, that the slave gets the better of the fight, and even flogs his master;* for which there is no law to punish him; but when the fight is over that is the last of it. So far as religious instruction is concerned, they have it on terms of equality, the bond and the free; they have no respect of persons, they have neither slave laws nor negro pews. Neither do they separate husbands and wives, nor parents and children. All things considered, if I must be a slave, I had by far, rather be a slave to an Indian, than to a white man, from the experience I have had with both.

A majority of the Indians were uneducated, and still followed up their old heathen traditional notions. They made it a rule to have an Indian dance or frolic, about once a fortnight; and they would come together far and near to attend these dances. They would most generally commence about the middle of the afternoon; and would give notice by the blowing of horns. One would commence blowing and another would answer, and so it would go all round the neighborhood. When a number had got together, they would strike a circle about twenty rods in circumference, and kindle up fires about twenty feet apart, all around, in this circle. In the centre they would have a large fire to dance around, and at each one of the small fires there would be a squaw to keep up the fire, which looked delightful off at a distance.

But the most degrading practice of all, was the

---

* This singular fact is corroborated in a letter read by the publisher, from an acquaintance while passing through this country in 1849.

use of intoxicating drinks, which were used to a
great excess by all that attended these stump dances.
At almost all of these fires there was some one with
rum to sell. There would be some dancing, some
singing, some gambling, some fighting, and some
yelling ; and this was kept up often for two days.
and nights together.

Their dress for the dance was most generally a
great bunch of bird feathers, coon tails, or something of the kind stuck in their heads, and a great
many shells tied about their legs to rattle while
dancing. Their manner of dancing is taking hold
of each others hands and forming a ring around the
large fire in the centre, and go stomping around it
until they would get drunk or their heads would
get to swimming, and then they would go off and
drink, and another set come on. Such were some
of the practises indulged in by these Indian slaveholders.

My last owner was in a declining state of health
when he bought me; and not long after he bought
me he went off forty or fifty miles from home to be
doctored by an Indian doctor, accompanied by his
wife. I was taken along also to drive the carriage
and to wait upon him during his sickness. But he
was then so feeble, that his life was of but short
duration after the doctor commenced on him.

While he lived, I waited on him according to the
best of my ability. I watched over him night and
day until he died, and even prepared his body for
the tomb, before I left him. He died about midnight and I understood from his friends that he was

not to be buried until the second day after his death. I pretended to be taking on at a great rate about his death, but I was more excited about running away, than I was about that, and before daylight the next morning I proved it, for I was on my way to Can-ada.

I never expected a better opportunity would present itself for my escape. I slipped out of the room as if I had gone off to weep for the deceased, knowing that they would not feel alarmed about me until after my master was buried and they had returned back to his residence. And even then, they would think that I was somewhere on my way home ; and it would be at least four or five days before they would make any stir in looking after me. By that time, if I had no bad luck, I should be out of much danger.

After the first day, I laid by in the day and traveled by night for several days and nights, passing in this way through several tribes of Indians. I kept pretty near the boundary line. I recollect getting lost one dark rainy night. Not being able to find the road I came into an Indian settlement at the dead hour of the night. I was wet, wearied, cold and hungry ; and yet I felt afraid to enter any of their houses or wigwams, not knowing whether they would be friendly or not. But I knew the Indians were generally drunkards, and that occasionally a drunken white man was found straggling among them, and that such an one would be more likely to find friends from sympathy than an upright man.

So I passed myself off that night as a drunkard among them. I walked up to the door of one of their houses, and fell up against it, making a great noise like a drunken man; but no one came to the door. I opened it and staggered in, falling about, and making a great noise. But finally an old woman got up and gave me a blanket to lie down on.

There was quite a number of them lying about on the dirt floor, but not one could talk or understand a word of the English language. I made signs so as to let them know that I wanted something to eat, but they had nothing, so I had to go without that night. I laid down and pretended to be asleep, but I slept none that night, for I was afraid that they would kill me if I went to sleep. About one hour before day, the next morning, three of the females got up and put into a tin kettle a lot of ashes with water, to boil, and then poured into it about one quart of corn. After letting it stand a few moments, they poured it into a trough, and pounded it into thin hominy. They washed it out, and boiled it down, and called me up to eat my breakfast of it.

After eating, I offered them six cents, but they refused to accept it. I then found my way to the main road, and traveled all that day on my journey, and just at night arrived at a public house kept by an Indian, who also kept a store. I walked in and asked if I could get lodging, which was granted; but I had not been there long before three men came riding up about dusk, or between sunset and dark. They were white men, and I supposed slaveholders.

At any rate when they asked if they could have
lodging, I trembled for fear they might be in pursuit
of me. But the landlord told them that he could
not lodge them, but they could get lodging about
two miles off, with a white man, and they turned
their horses and started.

The landlord asked me where I was traveling to,
and where I was from. I told him that I had been
out looking at the country; that I had thought of
buying land, and that I lived in the State of Ohio,
in the village of Perrysburgh. He then said that he
had lived there himself, and that he had acted as an
interpreter there among the Maumee tribe of Indians
for several years. He then asked who I was acquainted with there ? I informed him that I knew
Judge Hollister, Francis Hollister, J. W. Smith, and
others. At this he was so much pleased that he
came up and took me by the hand, and received me
joyfully, after seeing that I was acquainted with
those of his old friends.

I could converse with him understandingly from
personal acquaintance, for I had lived there when I
first ran away from Kentucky. But I felt it to be
my duty to start off the next morning before breakfast, or sunrise. I bought a dozen of eggs, and
had them boiled to carry with me to eat on the way.
I did not like the looks of those three men, and
thought I would get on as fast as possible for fear
I might be pursued by them.

I was then about to enter the territory of another
slave State, Missouri. I had passed through the
fiery ordeal of Sibley, Gatewood, and Garrison, and

had even slipped through the fingers of Deacon Whitfield. I had doubtless gone through great peril in crossing the Indian territory, in passing through the various half civilized tribes, who seemed to look upon me with astonishment as I passed along. Their hands were almost invariably filled with bows and arrows, tomahawks, guns, butcher knives, and all the various implements of death which are used by them. And what made them look still more frightful, their faces were often painted red, and their heads muffled with birds feathers, bushes, coons tails and owls heads. But all this I had passed through, and my long enslaved limbs and spirit were then in full stretch for emancipation. I felt as if one more short struggle would set me free.

CHAPTER XV

EARLY in the morning I left the Indian territory as I have already said, for fear I might be pursued by the three white men whom I had seen there over night; but I had not proceeded far before my fears were magnified a hundred fold.

I always dreaded to pass through a prairie, and on coming to one which was about six miles in width, I was careful to look in every direction to see whether there was any person in sight before I entered it; but I could see no one. So I started across with a hope of crossing without coming in contact with any one on the prairie. I walked as fast as I could, but when I got about midway of the prairie, I came to a high spot where the road forked, and three men came up from a low spot as if they had been there concealed. They were all on horse back, and I supposed them to be the same men that had tried to get lodging where I stopped over night. Had this been in timbered land, I might have stood some chance to have dodged them, but there I was, out in the open prairie, where I could see no possible way by which I could escape.

They came along slowly up behind me, and finally passed, and spoke or bowed their heads on passing, but they traveled in a slow walk and kept but a very few steps before me, until we got nearly across the prairie. When we were coming near a plantation a piece off from the road on the skirt of the timbered land, they whipped up their horses and left the road as if they were going across to this plantation. They soon got out of my sight by going down into a valley which lay between us and the plantation. Nôt seeing them rise the hill to go up to the farm, excited greater suspicion in my mind, so I stepped over on the brow of the hill, where I could see what they were doing, and to my surprise I saw them going right back in the direction they had just came, and they were going very fast. I was then satisfied that they were after me and that they were only going back to get more help to assist them in taking me, for fear that I might kill some of them if they undertook it. The first impression was that I had better leave the road immediately; so I bolted from the road and ran as fast as I could for some distance in the thick forest, and concealed myself for about fifteen or twenty minutes, which were spent in prayer to God for his protecting care and guidance.

My impression was that when they should start in pursuit of me again, they would follow on in the direction which I was going when they left me; and not finding or hearing of me on the road, they would come back and hunt through the woods

ʟ ʟ and. and if they could find no track they might
go and get dogs to trace me out.

I thought my chance of escape would be better,
if I went back to the same side of the road that
they first went, for the purpose of deceiving them ;
as I supposed that they would not suspect my going
in the same direction that they went, for the purpose of escaping from them.

So I traveled all that day square off from the
road through the wild forest without any knowledge of the country whatever; for I had nothing
to travel by but the sun by day, and the moon and
stars by night.   Just before night I came in sight of
a large plantation, where I saw quite a number of
horses running at large in a field, and knowing that
my success in escaping depended upon my getting
out of that settlement within twenty-four hours,
to save myself from everlasting slavery, I thought
I should be justified in riding one of those horses,
that night, if I could catch one.   I cut a grape
vine with my knife, and made it into a bridle ; and
shortly after dark I went into the field and tried
to catch one of the horses. · I got a bunch of dry
blades of fodder and walked up softly towards the
horses, calling to them " cope," "cope," "cope ;"
but there was only one out of the number that I
was able to get my hand on, and that was an old
mare, which I supposed to be the mother of all the
rest ; and I knew that I could walk faster than she
could travel.   She had a bell on and was very thin
in flesh ; she looked gentle and walked on three
legs only.   The young horses pranced and galloped

off. I was not able to get near them, and the old mare being of no use to me, I left them all. After fixing my eyes on the north star I pursued my journey, holding on to my bridle with a hope of finding a horse upon which I might ride that night.

I found a road leading pretty nearly in the direc-tion which I wanted to travel, and I kept it. After traveling several miles I found another large planta-tion where there was a prospect of finding a horse. I stepped up to the barn-yard, wherein I found several horses. There was a little barn standing with the door open, and I found it quite an easy task to get the horses into the barn, and select out the best looking one of them. I pulled down the fence, led the noble beast out and mounted him, taking a northern direction, being able to find a road which led that way. But I had not gone over three or four miles before I came to a large stream of water which was past fording; yet I could see that it had been forded by the road track, but from high water it was then impassible. As the horse seemed willing to go in I put him through; but before he got in far, he was in water up to his sides and finally the water came over his back and he swam over. I got as wet as could be, but the horse carried me safely across at the proper place. After I got out a mile or so from the river, I came into a large prairie, which I think must have been twenty or thirty miles in width, and the road run across it about in the direction that I wanted to go. I laid whip to the horse, and I think he must have carried me not less than forty miles that night, or before

sun rise the next morning. I then stopped him in
a spot of high grass in an old field, and took off the
bridle. I thanked God, and thanked the horse for
what he had done for me, and wished him a safe
journey back home.

I know the poor horse must have felt stiff, and
tired from his speedy jaunt, and I felt very bad myself, riding at that rate all night without a saddle;
but I felt as if I had too much at stake to favor
either horse flesh or man flesh. I could indeed afford to crucify my own flesh for the sake of redeem-
ing myself from perpetual slavery.

Some may be disposed to find fault with my taking the horse as I did; but I did nothing more than
nine out of ten would do if they were placed in the
same circumstances. I had no disposition to steal
a horse from any man. But I ask, if a white man
had been captured by the Cherokee Indians and carried away from his family for life into slavery, and
could see a chance to escape and get back to his family; should the Indians pursue him with a determination to take him back or take his life, would it be a
crime for the poor fugitive, whose life, liberty and
future happiness were all at stake, to mount any
man's horse by the way side, and ride him without
asking any questions, to effect his escape? Or who
would not do the same thing to rescue a wife, child,
father, or mother? Such an act committed by a
white man under the same circumstances would not
only be pronounced proper, but praiseworthy; and
if he neglected to avail himself of such a means of
escape he would be pronounced a fool. Therefore

from this act I have nothing to regret, for I have done nothing more than any other reasonable person would have done under the same circumstances. But I had good luck from the morning I left the horse until I got back into the State of Ohio. About two miles from where I left the horse, I found a public house on the road, where I stopped and took breakfast. Being asked where I was traveling, I replied that I was going home to Perrysburgh, Ohio, and that I had been out to look at the land in Missouri, with a view of buying. They supposed me to be a native of Ohio, from the fact of my being so well acquainted with its location, its principal cities, inhabitants, &c.

The next night I put up at one of the best hotels in the village where I stopped, and acted with as much independence as if I was worth a million of dollars; talked about buying land, stock and village property, and contrasting it with the same kind of property in the State of Ohio. In this kind of talk they were most generally interested, and I was treated just like other travelers. I made it a point to travel about thirty miles each day on my way to Jefferson city. On several occasions I have asked the landlords where I have stopped over night, if they could tell me who kept the best house where I would stop the next night, which was most generally in a small village. But for fear I might forget, I would get them to give me the name on a piece of paper as a kind of recommend. This would serve as an introduction through which I have always been well received from one landlord to another, and I have always stopped at the best houses, eaten at the first tables, and slept in the best beds. No man ever asked me whether I was bond or free, black or white, rich or poor; but I always presented a bold front and showed the best side out, which was all the pass I had. But when I got within about one hundred miles of Jefferson city, where I expected to take a Steamboat passage to St. Louis, I stopped over night at a hotel, where I met with a young white man who was traveling on to Jefferson City on horse back, and was also leading a horse with a saddle and bridle on.

I asked him if he would let me ride the horse which he was leading, as I was going to the same city? He said that it was a hired horse, that he was paying at the rate of fifty cents per day for it, but if I would pay the same I could ride him. I accepted the offer and we rode together to the city. We were on the road together two or three days stopped and ate and slept together at the same hotels.

CHAPTER XVI.

THE greatest of my adventures came off when I arrived at Jefferson City. There I expected to meet an advertisement for my person; it was there I must cross the river or take a steamboat down; it was there I expected to be interrogated and required to prove whether I was actually a free man or a slave. If I was free, I should have to show my free papers; and if I was a slave I should be required to tell who my master was.

I stopped at a hotel, however, and ascertained that there was a steamboat expected down the river that day for St. Louis. I also found out that there were several passengers at that house who were going down on board of the first boat. I knew that the captain of a steamboat could not take a colored passenger on board of his boat from a slave state without first ascertaining whether such person was bond or free; I knew that this was more than he would dare to do by the laws of the slave states —and now to surmount this difficulty it brought into exercise all the powers of my mind. I would have got myself boxed up as freight, and have been forwarded to St. Louis, but I had no friend that I could trust to do it for me. This plan has since been adopted by some with success. But finally I thought I might possibly pass myself off as a body servant to the passengers going from the hotel down.

So I went to a store and bought myself a large trunk, and took it to the hotel. Soon, a boat came in which was bound to St. Louis, and the passengers started down to get on board. I took up my large trunk, and started along after them as if I was their servant. My heart trembled in view of the dangerous experiment which I was then about to try. It required all the moral courage that I was master of to bear me up in view of my critical condition. The white people that I was following walked on board and I after them. I acted as if the trunk was full of clothes, but I had not a stitch of clothes in it. The passengers went up into the cabin and I followed them with the trunk. I suppose this made the captain think that I was their slave.

I not only took the trunk in the cabin but stood by it until after the boat had started as if it belonged to my owners, and I was taking care of it for them; but as soon as the boat got fairly under way, I knew that some account would have to be given of me; so I then took my trunk down on the deck among the deck passengers to prepare myself to meet the clerk of the boat, when he should come to collect fare from the deck passengers.

Fortunately for me there was quite a number of deck passengers on board, among whom there were many Irish. I insinuated myself among them so as to get into their good graces, believing that if I should get into a difficulty they would stand by me. I saw several of these persons going up to the saloon buying whiskey, and I thought this might be the most effectual way by which I could gain speedily their respect and sympathy. So I participated with them pretty freely for awhile, or at least until after I got my fare settled. I placed myself in a little crowd of them, and invited them all up to the bar with me, stating that it was my treat. This was responded to, and they walked up and drank and I footed the bill. This, of course, brought us into a kind of a union. We sat together and laughed and talked freely. Within ten or fifteen minutes I remarked that I was getting dry again, and invited them up and treated again. By this time I was thought to be one of the most liberal and gentlemanly men on board, by these deck passengers; they were ready to do any thing for me—they got to singing songs, and telling long yarns in which I took quite an active part; but it was all for effect.

By this time the porter came around ringing his bell for all passengers who had not paid their fare, to walk up to the captain's office and settle it. Some of my Irish friends had not yet settled, and I asked one of them if he would be good enough to take my money and get me a ticket when he was getting one for himself, and he quickly replied "yes sir, I will get you a tacket," So he relieved me of my greatest trouble. When they came round to gather the tickets before we got to St. Louis, my ticket was taken with the rest, and no questions were asked me.

The next day the boat arrived at St. Louis; my object was to take passage on board of the first boat which was destined for Cincinnati, Ohio; and as there was a boat going out that day for Pittsburgh, I went on board to make some inquiry about the fare &c., and found the steward to be a colored man with whom I was acquainted. He lived in Cincinnati, and had rendered me some assistance in making my escape to Canada, in the summer of 1838, and he also very kindly aided me then in getting back into a land of freedom. The swift running steamer started that afternoon on her voyage, which soon wafted my body beyond the tyrannical limits of chattel slavery. When the boat struck the mouth of the river Ohio, and I had once more the pleasure of looking on that lovely stream, my heart leaped up for joy at the glorious prospect that I should again be free. Every revolution of the mighty steam-engine seemed to bring me nearer and nearer the "promised land." Only a few days had elapsed, before I was permitted by the smiles of a good providence, once more to gaze on the green hill-tops and valleys of old Kentucky, the State of my nativity. And notwithstanding I was deeply interested while standing on the deck of the steamer looking at the beauties of nature on either side of the river, as she pressed her way up the stream, my very soul was pained to look upon the slaves in the fields of

Kentucky, still toiling under their task-masters without pay. It was on this soil I first breathed the free air of Heaven, and felt the bitter pangs of slavery—it was here that I first learned to abhor it. It was here I received the first impulse of human rights—it was here that I first entered my protest against the bloody institution of slavery, by running away from it, and declared that I would no longer work for any man as I had done, without wages.

When the steamboat arrived at Portsmouth, Ohio, I took off my trunk with the intention of going to Canada. But my funds were almost exhausted, so I had to stop and go to work to get money to travel on. I hired myself at the American Hotel to a Mr. McCoy to do the work of a porter, to black boots, &c., for which he was to pay me $12 per month. I soon found the landlord to be bad pay, and not only that, but he would not allow me to charge for blacking boots, although I had to black them after everbody had gone to bed at night, and set them in the barroom, where the gentlemen could come and get them in the morning while I was at other work. I had nothing extra for this, neither would he pay me my regular wages; so I thought this was a little too much like slavery, and devised a plan by which I got some pay for my work.

I made it a point never to blacken all the boots and shoes over night, neither would I put any of them in the bar-room, but lock them up in a room where no one could get them without calling for me. I got a piece of broken vessel, placed it in the room just before the boots, and put into it several pieces of small change, as if it had been given me for boot blacking ; and almost every one that came in after their boots, would throw some small trifle into my contribution box, while I was there blacking away. In this way, I made more than my landlord paid me, and I soon got a good stock of cash again. One morning I blacked a gentleman's boots who came in during the night by a steamboat. After he had put on his boots, I was called into the barroom to button his straps ; and while I was performing this service, not thinking to see anybody that knew me, I happened to look up at the man's face and who should it be but one of the very gamblers who had recently sold me. I dropped his foot and bolted from the room as if I had been struck by an electric shock. The man happened not to recognize me, but this strange conduct on my part excited the landlord, who followed me out to see what was the matter. He found me with my hand to my breast, groaning at a great rate. He asked me what was the matter ; but I was not able to inform him correctly, but said that I felt very bad indeed. He of course thought I was sick with the colic and ran in the house and got some hot stuff for me, with spice, ginger, &c. But I never got able to go into the bar-room until long after breakfast time, when I knew this man was gone ; then I got well.

And yet I have no idea that the man would have hurt a hair of my head ; but my first thought was that he was after me. I then made up my mind to leave Portsmouth; its location being right on the border of a slave State.

A short time after this a gentleman put up there over night named Smith, from Perrysburgh, with whom I was acquainted in the North. He was on his way to Kentucky to buy up a drove of fine horses, and he wanted me to go and help him to drive his horses out to Perrysburgh, and said he would pay all my expenses if I would go. So I made a contract to go and agreed to meet him the next week, on a set day, in Washington, Ky., to start with his drove to the north. Accordingly at the time I took a steamboat passage down to Maysville, near where I was to meet Mr. Smith with my trunk. When I arrived at Maysville, I found that Washington was still six miles back from the river. I stopped at a hotel and took my breakfast, and who should I see there but a captain of a boat, who saw me but two years previous going down the river Ohio with handcuffs on, in a chain gang ; but he happened not to know me. I left my trunk at the hotel and went out to Washington, where I found Mr. Smith, and learned that he was not going to start off with his drove until the next day.

The followig letter which was addressed to the committee to investigate the truth of my narrative, will explain this part of it to the reader and corroborate my statements :

MAUMEE CITY, April 5, 1845.
CHAS. H. STEWART, ESQ.

DEAR SIR:—Your favor of 13th February, addressed to me at Perrysburgh, was not received until yesterday ; having removed to this place the

letter was not forwarded as it should have been,   In
reply to your inquiry respecting Henry Bibb, I can
only say that about the year 1838 I became acquainted with him at Perrysbugh—employed him to do
some work by the job which he performed well, and
from his apparent honesty and candor, I became
much interested in him.   About that time he went
South for the purpose, as was said, of getting his
wife, who was there in slavery.   In the spring of
1841, I found him at Portsmouth on the Ohio river,
and after much persuasion, employed him to assist
my man to drive home some horses and cattle which
I was about purchasing near Maysville, Ky.   My
confidence in him was such that when about half
way home I separated the horses from the cattle,
and left him with the latter, with money and instructions to hire what help he wanted to get to Perrysburgh.   This he accomplished to my entire satisfaction.   He worked for me during the summer, and I
was unwilling to part with him, but his desire to go
to school and mature plans for the liberation of his
wife, were so strong that he left for Detroit, where
he could enjoy the society of his colored brethren.
I have heard his story and must say that I have
not the least reason to suspect it being otherwise
than true, and furthermore, I firmly believe, and
have for a long time, that he has the foundation to
make himself useful.   I shall always afford him all
the facilities in my power to assist him, until I hear
of something in relation to him to alter my mind.

  Yours in the cause of truth,

      J. W. SMITH.

When I arrived at Perrysburgh, I went to work for Mr. Smith for several months. This family I found to be one of the most kind-hearted, and un-prejudiced that I ever lived with. Mr. and Mrs. Smith lived up to their profession.

I resolved to go to Detroit, that winter, and go to school, in January 1842. But when I arrived at Detroit I soon found that I was not able to give myself a very thorough education. I was among strangers, who were not disposed to show me any great favors. I had every thing to pay for, and clothing to buy, so I graduated within three weeks ! And this was all the schooling that I have ever had in my life.

W. C. Monroe was my teacher ; to him I went about two weeks only. My occupation varied ac-cording to circumstances, as I was not settled in mind about the condition of my bereaved family for several years, and could not settle myself down at any permanent business. I saw occasionally, fugi-tives from Kentucky, some of whom I knew, but none of them were my relatives ; none could give me the information which I desired most.

CHAPTER XVII.

THE first direct information that I received concerning any of my relations, after my last escape from slavery, was communicated in a letter from Wm. H. Gatewood, my former owner, which I here insert word for word, without any correction :

BEDFORD, TRIMBLE COUNTY, KY.

Mr. H. BIBB.

DEAR SIR :—After my respects to you and yours &c., I received a small book which you sent to me that I peroseed and found it was sent by H. Bibb I am a stranger in Detroit and know no man there without it is Walton H. Bibb if this be the man please to write to me and tell me all about that place and the people I will tell you the news here as well as I can your mother is still living here and she is well the people are generally well in this cuntry times are dull and produce low give my compliments to King, Jack, and all my friends in that cuntry I read that book you sent me and think it will do very well—George is sold, I do not know any thing about him I have nothing more at present, but remain yours &c

W. H GATEWOOD.

February 9th, 1844.

P. S. You will please to answer this letter.

Never was I more surprised than at the reception of this letter, it came so unexpected to me. There had just been a State Convention held in Detroit, by the free people of color, the proceedings of which were published in pamphlet form. I forwarded several of them to distinguished slaveholders in Kentucky—one among others was Mr. Gatewood, and gave him to understand who sent it. After showing this letter to several of my anti-slavery friends, and asking their opinions about the proprie-ty of my answering it, I was advised to do it, as Mr. Gatewood had no claim on me as a slave, for he had sold and got the money for me and my family. So I wrote him an answer, as near as I can recollect, in the following language :

"DEAR SIR :—I am happy to inform you that you are not mistaken in the man whom you sold as pro perty, and received pay for as such. But I thank God that I am not property now, but am regarded as a man like yourself, and although I live far north, I am enjoying a comfortable living by my own in-dustry. If you should ever chance to be traveling this way, and will call on me, I will use you better than you did me while you held me as a slave. Think not that I have any malice against you, for the cruel treatment which yoı inflicted on me while I was in your power. As it was the custom of your country, to treat your fellow men as you did me and my little family, I can freely forgive you.

I wish to be remembered in love to my aged mother, and friends; please tell her that if we should never meet again in this life, my prayer shall be to God that we may meet in Heaven, where parting shall be no more.

"You wish to be remembered to King and Jack. I am pleased, sir, to inform you that they are both here, well, and doing well. They are both living in Canada West. They are now the owners of better farms than the men are who once owned them.

You may perhaps think hard of us for running away from slavery, but as to myself, I have but one apology to make for it, which is this: I have only to regret that I did not start at an earlier period. I might have been free long before I was. But you had it in your power to have kept me there much longer than you did. I think it is very probable that I should have been a toiling slave on your plantation to-day, if you had treated me differently.

To be compelled to stand by and see you whip and slash my wife without mercy, when I could afford her no protection, not even by offering myself to suffer the lash in her place, was more than I felt it to be the duty of a slave husband to endure, while the way was open to Canada. My infant child was also frequently flogged by Mrs. Gatewood, for crying, until its skin was bruised literally purple. This kind of treatment was what drove me from home and family, to seek a better home for them. But I am willing to forget the past. I should be pleased to hear from you again, on the reception of this, and should also be very happy to correspond with you often, if it should be agreeable to yourself. I subscribe myself a friend to the oppressed, and Liberty forever.   HENRY BIBB.

  WILLIAM GATEWOOD.

Detroit, March 23d, 1844.

The first time that I ever spoke before a public audience, was to give a narration of my own sufferings and adventures, connected with slavery. I commenced in the village of Adrian, State of Michigan, May, 1844. From that up to the present period, the principle part of my time has been faithfully devoted to the cause of freedom—nerved up and encouraged by the sympathy of anti-slavery friends on the one hand, and prompted by a sense of duty to my enslaved countrymen on the other, especially, when I remembered that slavery had robbed me of my freedom—deprived me of education—banished me from my native State, and robbed me of my family.

I went from Michigan to the State of Ohio, where I traveled over some of the Southern counties of that State, in company with Samuel Brooks, and Amos Dresser, lecturing upon the subject of American Slavery. The prejudice of the people at that time was very strong against the abolitionists; so much so that they were frequently mobbed for dis cussing the subject.

We appointed a series of meetings along on the Ohio River, in sight of the State of Virginia; and in several places we had Virginians over to hear us upon the subject. I recollect our having appointed a meeting in the city of Steubenville, which is situated on the bank of the river Ohio. There was but one known abolitionist living in that city, named George Ore. On the day of our meeting, when we arrived in this splendid city there was not a church, school house, nor hall, that we could get for love or money, to hold our meeting in. Finally, I believe that the whigs consented to let us have the use of their club room, to hold the meeting in; but before the hour had arrived for us to commence, they re-considered the matter, and informed us that we could not have the use of their house for an abolition meeting.

We then got permission to hold forth in the public market house, and even then so great was the hostility of the rabble, that they tried to bluff us off, by threats and epithets. Our meeting was advertised to take place at nine o'clock, A. M. The pro-slavery parties hired a colored man to take a large auction bell, and go all over the city ringing it, and crying, " ho ye! ho ye! Negro auction to take place in the market house, at nine o'clock, by George Ore!" This cry was sounded all over the city, which called out many who would not otherwise have been present. They came to see if it was really the case. The object of the rabble in having the bell rung was, to prevent us from attempting to speak. But at the appointed

hour, Bro. Dresser opened the meeting with prayer
and Samuel Brooks mounted the block and spoke
for fifteen or twenty minutes, after which Mr.
Dresser took the block and talked about one hour
upon the wickedness of slaveholding. There were
not yet many persons present. They were standing
off I suppose to see if I was to be offered for sale.
Many windows were hoisted and store doors open,
and they were looking and listening to what was said.
After Mr. Dresser was through, I was called to take
the stand. Just at this moment there was no small
stir in rushing forward; so much indeed, that I
thought they were coming up to mob me. I should
think that in less than fifteen minutes there were
about one thousand persons standing around, listening. I saw many of them shedding tears while I
related the sad story of my wrongs. At twelve
o'clock we adjourned the meeting, to meet again at
the same place at two P. M. Our afternoon meeting was well attended until nearly sunset, at which
time, we saw some signs of a mob and adjourned.
The mob followed us that night to the house of Mr.
Ore, and they were yelling like tigers, until late that
night, around the house, as if they wanted to tear it
down.

In the fall of 1844, S. B. Treadwell, of Jackson,
and myself, spent two or three months in lecturing
through the State of Michigan, upon the abolition
of slavery, in a section of country where abolitionists
were few and far between. Our meetings were generally appointed in small log cabins, school houses,
among the farmers, which were some times crowded

full ; and where they had no horse teams, it was often the case that there would be four or five ox teams come, loaded down with men, women and children, to attend our meetings.

But the people were generally poor, and in many places not able to give us a decent night's lodging. We most generally carried with us a few pounds of candles to light up the houses wherein we held our meetings after night ; for in many places, they had neither candles nor candlesticks. After meeting was out, we have frequently gone from three to eight miles to get lodging, through the dark forest, where there was scarcely any road for a wagon to run on.

I have traveled for miles over swamps, where the roads were covered with logs, without any dirt over them, which has sometimes shook and jostled the wagon to pieces, where we could find no shop or any place to mend it. We would have to tie it up with bark, or take the lines to tie it with, and lead the horse by the bridle. At other times we were in mud up to the hubs of the wheels. I recollect one evening, we lectured in a little village where there happened to be a Southerner present, who was a personal friend of Deacon Whitfield, who became much offended at what I said about his " Bro. Whitfield," and complained about it after the meeting was out.

He told the people not to believe a word that I said, that it was all a humbug. They asked him how he knew ?   " Ah! " said he, " he has slandered Bro. Whitfield. I am well acquainted with him, we both belonged to one church ; and Whitfield is

one of the most respectable men in all that region
of country." They asked if he (Whitfield) was a
slaveholder ?

The reply was "yes, but he treated his slaves
well."

" Well," said one, "that only próves that he has
told us the truth ; for all we wish to know, is that
there is such a man as Whitfield, as represented by
Bibb, and that he is a slave holder."

On the 2d Sept., 1847, I started from Toledo on
board the canal packet Erie, for Cincinnati, Ohio.
But before going on board, I was waited on by one
of the boat's crew, who gave me a card of the
boat, upon which was printed, that no pains would
be spared to render all passengers comfortable who
might favor them with their patronage to Cincinnati. This card I slipped into my pocket, supposing it might be of some use to me. There were
several drunken loafers on board going through as
passengers, one of whom used the most vulgar
language in the cabin, where there were ladies, and
even vomited! But he was called a white man, and
a southerner, which made it all right. I of course
took my place in the cabin with the rest, and there
was nothing said against it that night. When the
passengers went forward to settle their fare I paid
as much as any other man, which entitled me to
the same privileges. The next morning at the
ringing of the breakfast bell, the proprietor of the
packet line, Mr. Samuel Doyle, being on board, invited the passengers to sit up to breakfast. He
also invited me personally to sit up to the table.

But after we were all seated, and some had began to eat, he came and ordered me up from the table, and said I must wait until the rest were done.

I left the table without making any reply, and walked out on the deck of the boat. After breakfast the passengers came up, and the cabin boy was sent after me to come to breakfast, but I refused. Shortly after, this man who had ordered me from the table, came up with the ladies. I stepped up and asked him if he was the captain of the boat. His answer was no, that he was one of the proprietors. I then informed him that I was going to leave his boat at the first stopping place, but before leaving I wanted to ask him a few questions: " Have I misbehaved to any one on board of this boat ? Have I disobeyed any law of this boat ?

" No," said he.

Have I not paid you as much as any other passenger through to Cincinnati ?"

" Yes," said he,

" Then I am sure that I have been insulted and imposed upon, on board of this boat, without any just cause whatever."

" No one has misused you, for you ought to have known better than to have come to the table where there were white people."

" Sir, did you not ask me to come to the table ?"

" Yes, but I did not know that you was a colored man, when I asked you ; and then it was better to insult one man than all the passengers on board of the boat."

Sir, I do not believe that there is a gentleman or

lady on board of this boat who would have considered it an insult for me to have taken my breakfast, and you have imposed upon me by taking my
money and promising to use me well, and then to
insult me as you have."

" I don't want any of your jaw," said he.

" Sir, with all due respect to your elevated station,
you have imposed upon me in a way which is un-
becoming a gentleman. I have paid my money, and
behaved myself as well as any other man, and I am
determined that no man shall impose on me as you
have, by deceiving me, without my letting the world
know it. I would rather a man should rob me of
my money at midnight, than to take it in that way."

I left this boat at the first stopping place, and
took the next boat to Cincinnati. On the last boat
I had no cause to complain of my treatment. When
I arrived at Cincinnati, I published a statement of
this affair in the Daily Herald.

The next day Mr. Doyle called on the editor in a
great passion.—" Here," said he, " what does this
mean."

" What, sir ?" said the editor quietly.

" Why, the stuff here, read it and see."

" Read it yourself," answered the editor.

" Well, I want to know if you sympathize with
this nigger here."

" Who, Mr. Bibb ? Why yes, I think he is a gentleman, and should be used as such."

" Why this is all wrong—all of it."

"Put your finger on the place, and I will right it."

" Well, he says that we took his money, when we

paid part back.   And if you take his part, why I'll
have nothing to do with your paper."

So ended his wrath.

In 1845, the anti-slavery friends of Michigan employed me to take the field as an anti-slavery Lecturer, in that State, during the Spring, Summer, and
Fall, pledging themselves to restore to me my wife
and child, if they were living, and could be
reached by human agency, which may be seen by the
following circular from the Signal of Liberty:

TO LIBERTY FRIENDS:—In the Signal of the
28th inst. is a report from the undersigned respecting Henry Bibb.   His narrative always excites deep
sympathy for himself and favorable bias for the
cause, which seeks to abolish the evils he so powerfully portrays.   Friends and foes attest his effi-
ciency.

Mr. Bibb has labored much in lecturing, yet has
collected but a bare pittance.   He has received from
Ohio lucrative offers, but we have prevailed on him
to remain in this State.

We think that a strong obligation rests on the
friends in this State to sustain Mr. Bibb, and restore
to him his wife and child.   Under the expectation
that Michigan will yield to these claims : will support their laborer, and re-unite the long severed ties
of husband and wife, parent and child, Mr. Bibb will
lecture through the whole State.

Our object is to prepare friends for the visit of
Mr. Bibb, and to suggest an effective mode of opera-
tions for the whole State.

Let friends in each vicinity appoint a collector—pay to him all contributions for the freedom of Mrs. Bibb and child : then transmit them to us.   We will acknowledge them in the Signal, and be responsible for them.   We will see that the proper measures for the freedom of Mrs. Bibb and child are taken, and if it be within our means we will accomplish it—nay we will accomplish it, if the objects be living and the friends sustain us.   But should we fail, the contributions will be held subject to the order of the donors, less however, by a proportionate deduction of expenses from each.

The hope of this re-union will nerve the heart and body of Mr. Bibb to re-doubled effort in a cause otherwise dear to him.   And as he will devote his whole time systematically to the anti-slavery cause he must also depend on friends for the means of livelihood.   We bespeak for him your hospitality, and such pecuniary contributions as you can afford, trusting that the latter may be sufficient to enable him to keep the field.

A. L. PORTER,
C. H. STEWART,
SILAS M. HOLMES

DETROIT, APRIL 22, 1845.

I have every reason to believe that they acted faithfully in the matter, but without success.   They wrote letters in every quarter where they would be likely to gain any information respecting her.   There were also two men sent from Michigan in the summer of 1845, down South, to find her if possible, and report—and whether they found out her condition, and refused to report, I am not able to say—but suffice it to say that they never have reported. They were respectable men and true friends of the cause, one of whom was a Methodist minister, and the other a cabinet maker, and both white men.

The small spark of hope which had still lingered about my heart had almost become extinct.

CHAPTER XVIII.

My last effort to recover my family.—Sad tidings of my wife.—
Her degradation.—I am compelled to regard our relation as dissolved forever.

In view of the failure to hear any thing of my wife,
many of my best friends advised me to get married
again, if I could find a suitable person. They regarded my former wife as dead to me, and all had
been done that could be.

But I was not yet satisfied myself, to give up. I
wanted to know certainly what had become of her.
So in the winter of 1845, I resolved to go back to
Kentucky, my native State, to see if I could hear
anything from my family. And against the advice
of all my friends, I went back to Cincinnati, where
I took passage on board of a Southern steamboat
to Madison, in the State of Indiana, which was only
ten miles from where Wm. Gatewood lived, who
was my former owner. No sooner had I landed in
Madison, than I learned, on inquiry, and from good
authority, that my wife was living in a state of
adultery with her master, and had been for the last
three years. This message she sent back to Kentucky, to her mother and friends. She also spoke
of the time and nanner of our separation by Deacon
Whitfield, my being taken off by the Southern black

legs, to where she knew not ; and that she had finally given me up. The child she said was still with her. Whitfield had sold her to this man for the above pur- poses at a high price, and she was better used than ordinary slaves. This was a death blow to all my hopes and pleasant plans. While I was in Madi- son I hired a white man to go over to Bedford, in Kentucky, where my mother was then living, and bring her over into a free State to see me. I hailed her approach with unspeakable joy. She informed me too, on inquiring whether my fam- ily had ever been heard from, that the report which I had just heard in relation to Malinda was substantially true, for it was the same message that she had sent to her mother and friends. And my mother thought it was no use for me to run any more risks, or to grieve myself any more about her.

From that time I gave her up into the hands of an all-wise Providence. As she was then living with another man, I could no longer regard her as my wife. After all the sacrifices, sufferings, and risks which I had run, striving to rescue her from the grasp of slavery ; every prospect and hope was cut off. She has ever since been regarded as theo- retically and practically dead to me as a wife, for she was living in a state of adultery, according to the law of God and man.

Poor unfortunate woman, I bring no charge of guilt against her, for I know not all the circum- stances connected with the case. It is consistent with slavery, however, to suppose that she became reconciled to it, from the fact of her sending word

back to her friends and relatives that she was much
better treated than she had ever been before, and
that she had also given me up.   It is also reasonable to suppose that there might have been some kind
of attachment formed by living together in this way
for years; and it is quite probable that they have
other children according to the law of nature, which
would have a tendency to unite them stronger together.

In view of all the facts and circumstances connected with this matter, I deem further comments
and explanations unnecessary on my part.   Finding
myself thus isolated in this peculiarly unnatural
state, I resolved, in 1846, to spend my days in traveling, to advance the anti-slavery cause.   I spent
the summer in Michigan, but in the subsequent fall
I took a trip to New England, where I spent the
winter.   And there I found a kind reception where-
ever I traveled among the friends of freedom.

While traveling about in this way among strangers, I was sometimes sick, with no permanent home,
or bosom friend to sympathise or take that care of
me which an affectionate wife would.   So I conceived the idea that it would be better for me to change
my position, provided I should find a suitable person.

In the month of May, 1847, I attended the anti-
slavery anniversary in the city of New York, where
I had the good fortune to be introduced to the favor
of a Miss Mary E. Miles, of Boston ; a lady whom I
had frequently heard very highly spoken of, for her
activity and devotion to the anti-slavery cause, as

well as her talents and learning, and benevolence in the cause of reforms, generally. I was very much impressed with the personal appearance of Miss Miles, and was deeply interested in our first interview, because I found that her principles and my own were nearly one and the same. I soon found by a few visits, as well as by letters, that she possessed moral principle, and frankness of disposition, which is often sought for but seldom found. These, in connection with other amiable qualities, soon won my entire confidence and affection. But this secret I kept to myself until I was fully satisfied that this feeling was reciprocal ; that there was indeed a congeniality of principles and feeling, which time nor eternity could never change.

When I offered myself for matrimony, we mutually engaged ourselves to each other, to marry in one year, with this condition, viz : that if either party should see any reason to change their mind within that time, the contract should not be considered binding. We kept up a regular correspondence during the time, and in June, 1848, we had the happiness to be joined in holy wedlock. Not in slaveholding style, which is a mere farce, without the sanction of law or gospel ; but in accordance with the laws of God and our country. My beloved wife is a bosom friend, a help-meet, a loving companion in all the social, moral, and religious relations of life. She is to me what a poor slave's wife can never be to her husband while in the condition of a s_ave; for she can not be true to her husband contrary to the will of her master. She can neither be pure nor virtuous, contrary to the will of her master. She dare not refuse to be reduced to a state of adultery at the will of her master ; from the fact that the slaveholding law, customs and teachings are all against the poor slaves.

I presume there are no class of people in the United States who so highly appreciate the legality of marriage as those persons who have been held and treated as property. Yes, it is that fugitive who knows from sad experience, what it is to have his wife tyrannically snatched from his bosom by a slaveholding professor of religion, and finally reduced to a state of adultery, that knows how to appreciate the law that repels such high-handed villany. Such as that to which the writer has been exposed. But thanks be to God, I am now free from the hand of the cruel oppressor, no more to be plundered of my dearest rights ; the wife of my bosom, and my poor unoffending offspring. Of Malinda I will only add a word in conclusion. The relation once subsisting between us, to which I clung, hoping against hope, for years, after we were torn assunder, not having been sanctioned by any loyal power, cannot be cancelled by a legal process. Voluntarily assumed without law mutually, it was by her relinquished years ago without my knowledge, as before named ; during which time I was making every effort to secure her restoration. And it was not until after living alone in the world for more than eight years without a companion known in law or morals, that I changed my condition.

CHAPTER XIX.

Comments on S. Gatewood's letter about slaves stealing.—Their conduct vindicated.—Comments on W. Gatewood's letter.

BUT it seems that I am not now beyond the reach of the foul slander of slaveholders. They are not satisfied with selling and banishing me from my native State. As soon as they got news of my being in the free North, exposing their peculiar Institution, a libelous letter was written by Silas Gatewood of Kentucky, a son of one of my former owners, to a Northern Committee, for publication, which he thought would destroy my influence and character. This letter will be found in the introduction.

He has charged me with the awful crime of taking from my keeper and oppressor, some of the fruits of my own labor for the benefit of myself and family.

But while writing this letter he seems to have overlooked the disgraceful fact that he was guilty himself of what would here be regarded highway robbery, in his conduct to me as narrated on page 87 of this narrative.

A word in reply to Silas Gatewood's letter. I am willing to admit all that is true, but shall deny that which is so basely false. In the first place, he

8

puts words in my mouth that I never used. He says that I represented that " my mother belonged to James Bibb." I deny ever having said so in private or public. He says that I stated that Bibb's daughter married a Sibley. I deny it. He also says that the first time that I left Kentucky for my liberty, I was gone about two years, before I went back to rescue my family. I deny it. I was gone from Dec. 25th, 1837, to May, or June, 1838. He says that I went back the second time for the purpose of taking off my family, and eight or ten more slaves to Canada. This I will not pretend to deny. He says I was guilty of disposing of articles from the farm for my own use, and pocketing the money, and that his father caught me stealing a sack full of wheat. I admit the fact. I acknowledge the wheat.

And who had a better right to eat of the fruits of my own hard earnings than myself? Many a long summer's day have I toiled with my wife and other slaves, cultivating his father's fields, and gathering in his harvest, under the scorching rays of the sun, without half enough to eat, or clothes to wear, and at the same time his meat-house was filled with bacon and bread stuff; his dairy with butter and cheese; his barn with grain, husbanded by the unrequited toil of the slaves. And yet if a slave presumed to take a little from the abundance which he had made by his own sweat and toil, to supply the demands of nature, to quiet the craving appetite which is sometimes almost irresistible, it is called stealing by slaveholders.

But I did not regard it as stealing then, I do not regard it as such now. I hold that a slave has a moral right to eat drink and wear all that he needs, and that it would be a sin on his part to suffer and starve in a country where there is a plenty to eat and wear within his reach. I consider that I had a just right to what I took, because it was the labor of my own hands. Should I take from a neighbor as a freeman, in a free country, I should consider myself guilty of doing wrong before God and man. But was I the slave of Wm. Gatewood to-day, or any other slaveholder, working without wages, and suffering with hunger or for clothing, I should not stop to inquire whether my master would approve of my helping myself to what I needed to eat or wear. For while the slave is regarded as property, how can he steal from his master? It is contrary to the very nature of the relation existing between master and slave, from the fact that there is no law to punish a slave for theft, but lynch law; and the way they avoid that is to hide well. For illustration, a slave from the State of Virginia, for cruel treatment left the State between daylight and dark, being borne off by one of his master's finest horses, and finally landed in Canada, where the British laws recognise no such thing as property in a human being. He was pursued by his owners, who expected to take advantage of the British law by claiming him as a fugitive from justice, and as such he was arrested and brought before the court of Queen's Bench. They swore that he was, at a certain time, the slave of Mr. A., and that he ran

away at such a time and stole and brought off a
horse. They enquired who the horse belonged to,
and it was ascertained that the slave and horse both
belonged to the same person. The court therefore
decided that the horse and the man were both recognised, in the State of Virginia, alike, as articles
of property, belonging to the same person—therefore, if there was theft committed on either side, the
former must have stolen off the latter—the horse
brought away the man, and not the man the horse.
So the man was discharged and pronounced free ac
cording to the laws of Canada. There are several
other letters published in this work upon the same
subject, from slaveholders, which it is hardly necessary for me to notice. However, I feel thankful
to the writers for the endorsement and confirmation
which they have given to my story. No matter
what their motives were, they have done me and the
anti-slavery cause good service in writing those letters—but more especially the Gatewood's. Silas
Gatewood has done more for me than all the rest.
He has labored so hard in his long communication
in trying to expose me, that he has proved every
thing that I could have asked of him ; and for which
I intend to reward him by forwarding him one of
my books, hoping that it may be the means of con-
verting him from a slaveholder to an honest man,
and an advocate of liberty for all mankind.

The reader will see in the introduction that Wm.
Gatewood writes a more cautious letter upon the
subject than his son Silas. " It is not a very easy
matter to catch old birds with chaff," and I presume

if Silas had the writing of his letter over again, he would not be so free in telling all he knew, and even more, for the sake of making out a strong case. The object of his writing such a letter will doubtless be understood by the reader. It was to destroy public confidence in the victims of slavery, that the system might not be exposed—it was to gag a poor fugitive who had undertaken to plead his own cause and that of his enslaved brethren. It was a feeble attempt to suppress the voice of universal freedom which is now thundering on every gale. But thank God it is too late in the day.

> Go stop the mighty thunder's roar,
> Go hush the ocean's sound,
> Or upward like the eagle soar
> To skies' remotest bound.
>
> And when thou hast the thunder stopped,
> And hushed the ocean's waves,
> Then, freedom's spirit bind in chains,
> And ever hold us slaves.
>
> And when the eagle's boldest feat,
> Thou canst perform with skill,
> Then, think to stop proud freedom's march
> And hold the bondman still.

CHAPTER XX.

Review of my narrative.—Licentiousness a prop of slavery.—A case of mild slavery given.—Its revolting features.—Times or my purchase and sale by professed Christians.—Concluding remarks.

I now conclude my narrative, by reviewing briefly what I have written. This little work has been written without any personal aid or a knowledge of the English grammer, which must in part be my apology for many of its imperfections.

I find in several places, where I have spoken out the deep feelings of my soul, in trying to describe the horrid treatment which I have so often received at the hands of slaveholding professors of religion, that I might possibly make a wrong impression on the minds of some northern freemen, who are unacquainted theoretically or practically with the customs and treatment of American slaveholders to their slaves. I hope that it may not be supposed by any, that I have exaggerated in the least, for the purpose of making out the system of slavery worse than it really is, for, to exaggerate upon the cruelties of this system, would be almost impossible ; and to write herein the most horrid features of it would not be in good taste for my book.

I have long thought from what has fallen under

my own observation while a slave, that the strongest reason why southerners stick with such tenacity
to their "peculiar instiution," is because licentious
white men could not carry out their wicked purposes among the defenceless colored population as
they now do, without being exposed and punished
by law, if slavery was abolished.   Female virtue
could not be trampled under foot with impunity,
and marriage among the people of color kept in
utter obscurity.

On the other hand, lest it should be said by
slaveholders and their apologists, that I have not
done them the justice to give a sketch of the best
side of slavery, if there can be any best side to it ,
therefore in conclusion, they may have the benefit
of the following case, that fell under the observation of the writer.   And I challenge America to
show a milder state of slavery than this.   I once
knew a Methodist in the state of Ky., by the name
of Young, who was the owner of a large number
of slaves, many of whom belonged to the same
church with their master.   They worshipped together in the same church.

Mr. Young never was known to flog one of his
slaves or sell one.   He fed and clothed them well,
and never over-worked them.   He allowed each
family a small house to themselves with a little
garden spot, whereon to raise their own vegetables ;
and a part of the day on Saturdays was allowed
them to cultivate it.

In process of time he became deeply involved in
debt by endorsing notes, and his property was all

advertised to be sold by the sheriff at public auction. It consisted in slaves, many of whom were his brothers and sisters in the church.

On the day of sale there were slave traders and speculators on the ground to buy. The slaves were offered on the auction block one after another until they were all sold before their old master's face. The first man offered on the block was an old gray-headed slave by the name of Richard. His wife followed him up to the block, and when they had bid him up to seventy or eighty dollars one of the bidders asked Mr. Young what he could do, as he looked very old and infirm? Mr. Young replied by saying, " he is not able to accomplish much manual labor, from his extreme age and hard labor in early life. Yet I would rather have him than many of those who are young and vigorous; who are able to perform twice as much labor—because I know him to be faithful and trustworthy, a Christian in good standing in my church. I can trust him anywhere with confidence. He has toiled many long years on my plantation and I have always found him faithful.

This giving him a good Christian character caused them to run him up to near two hundred dollars. His poor old companion stood by weeping and pleading that they might not be separated. But the marriage relation was soon dissolved by the sale, and they were separated never to meet again.

Another man was called up whose wife followed him with her infant in her arms, beseeching to be sold with her husband, which proved to be all in

vain. After the men were all sold they then se d
the women and children. They ordered the first
woman to lay down her child and mount the auction
block ; she refused to give up her little one and
clung to it as long as she could, while the cruel
lash was applied to her back for disobedience. She
pleaded for mercy in the name of God. But the
child was torn from the arms of its mother amid
the most heart rending-shrieks from the mother and
child on the one hand, and bitter oaths and cruel
lashes from the tyrants on the other. Finally the
poor little child was torn from the mother while
she was sacrificed to the highest bidder. In this
way the sale was carried on from begining to
end.

There was each speculator with his hand-cuffs to
bind his victims after the sale ; and while they
were doing their writings, the Christian portion of
the slaves asked permission to kneel in prayer on
the ground before they separated, which was granted.
And while bathing each other with tears of sorrow
on the verge of their final separation, their eloquent
appeals in prayer to the Most High seemed to
cause an unpleasant sensation upon the ears of their
tyrants, who ordered them to rise and make ready
their limbs for the caffles. And as they happened
not to bound at the first sound, they were soon
raised from their knees by the sound of the lash,
and the rattle of the chains, in which they were
soon taken off by their respective masters,—husbands from wives, and children from parents, never
expecting to meet until the judgment of the great

day. Then Christ shall say to the slaveholding
professors of religion, "Inasmuch as ye did it
unto one of the least of these little ones, my brethren, ye did it unto me."

Having thus tried to show the best side of slavery
that I can conceive of, the reader can exercise his
own judgment in deciding whether a man can be a
Bible Christian, and yet hold his Christian brethren
as property, so that they may be sold at any time
in market, as sheep or oxen, to pay his debts.

During my life in slavery I have been sold by
professors of religion several times. In 1836 "Bro."
Albert G. Sibley, of Bedford, Kentucky, sold me
for $850 to "Bro." John Sibley; and in the same year
he sold me to " Bro." Wm. Gatewood of Bedford, for
$850. In 1839 "Bro." Gatewood sold me to Madison
Garrison, a slave trader, of Louisville, Kentucky,
with my wife and child—at a depreciated price because I was a runaway.   In the same year he sold
me with my family to "Bro." Whitfield, in the city of
New Orleans, for $1200.   In 1841 "Bro." Whitfield
sold me from my family to Thomas Wilson and Co.,
blacklegs.   In the same year they sold me to a
" Bro." in the Indian Territory.   I think he was a
member of the Presbyterian Church.   F. E. Whitfield was a deacon in regular standing in the
Baptist Church. A. Sibley was a Methodist exhorter of the M. E. Church in good standing.   J.
Sibley was a class-leader in the same church; and
Wm. Gatewood was also an acceptable member of
the same church.

Is this Christianity ?   Is it honest or right ?   Is

it doing as we would be done by ? Is it in accord
ance with the principles of humanity or justice ?

I believe slaveholding to be a sin against God
and man under all circumstances. I have no sympathy with the person or persons who tolerate and
support the system willingly and knowingly, mo-
rally, religiously or politically.

Prayerfully and earnestly relying on the power
of truth, and the aid of the divine providence, I
trust that this little volume will bear some humble
part in lighting up the path of freedom and revo-
lutionizing public opinion upon this great subject.
And I here pledge myself, God being my helper, ever
to contend for the natural equality of the human
family, without regard to color, which is but fading
matter, while *mind* makes the man.

NEW YORK CITY, *May* 1, 1849.

HENRY BIBB.

OPINIONS OF THE PRESS.

From the many favorable notices of the Press which this
volume has received the following have been selected :

From the New York Evangelist.

"It will be difficult for any reader, however suspicious o
narratives of this kind, to resist the conviction which the sim
plicity, candor and good feeling of this work produces, of it;
entire truthfulness. And if true, what a history it depicts
Such oppression, fear, and suffering ; such courage and energy ;
such meek endurance and perseverance, could only be exempli-
fied by one whose nature was taxed to the uttermost. The hardest
task the reader will find is to suppress his indignation, and to
keep the balance of his judgment in reference to a system which
can possibly lead to such monstrous results. We wish the book
might obtain a universal perusal. It is adapted to produce the
right kind of feeling—a feeling of deep and abiding sympath
for the oppressed. We are all too indifferent to the wrong; or
the slave. We do not make his case our own. We do not feel
for those in bonds as bound with them. There is a lamentable
lack of proper Christian sympathy; and it is one of the best results of a book like this, that it quickens the flow of feeling, and
touches the heart. Mr. Bibb has manifested by a blameless life,
and by extraordinary talents, a character which not only co
roborates the truth of his history, but powerfully illustrates the
terrible nature of the system whose oppressions he here record
For his sake, as well as for the sake of humanity and freedom,
we hope an extensive sale awaits the little volume. It is small
neatly printed, and sold at a low price—from fifty cents to
seventy-five cents per copy. Let there be a little Christian
generosity exhibited in the sale of the work."

From the Liberator.

"Henry Bibb, the well known fugitive slave, has just published, in elegant style and with sundry pictorial illustrations,
a Narrative of his Life and Adventures, written by himself, and
remarkably well-written too ; with an Introduction by Lucius
: Matlack. Of all the narratives that have been published, e

one exceeds this in thrilling interest ; and of all the subjects of
them, no one appears to have seen and suffered so much as Mr.
Bibb. It is a book for the rising generation in particular ; and
we could wish that as many copies of it might be sold during
the present year, as there are slaves in the United States."

From the True Wesleyan.

" This is a volume of 204 pages, handsomely printed on good
paper and well bound. But it is not in the execution that the interest lies ; it is in the thrilling incidents so well told. We have
never been a great reader of novels, as all must know by our style
of writing, yet we have read enough to know the almost resistless
power which a well-executed tale, when once we commence reading, exerts over the mind, until we reach the end ; and did we not
know the author, and know from the best of proof that the book
is a true narrative, on reading it we should pronounce it a novel.
The reader may rely upon its truth, and yet he will find it so
full of touching incidents, daring adventures, and hair-breadth
escapes, that he will find his attention held spell-bound, from the
time he begins until he has finished the little volume. We think
the work cannot fail to meet with an extensive sale."

From the New York Tribune.

" This is a Narrative of intense interest. The author is well
known as a powerful speaker, keen in debate, shrewd in argument, and dangerous in retort. He here shows an equally ready
command of the pen, and has produced a book which would do
credit to a practiced writer. No stronger proof of the absurdity
of slavery can be demanded than this little history. By ap-
pealing to the sense of justice and the feeling of sympathy in
this artless record of a noble struggle with oppression and outrage, Mr. Bibb will make an impression on many readers, who
would not be reached by more elaborate statements. His book
has the attraction of a romance, though there was no romance in
his sufferings. They were matter of fact realities of the stern-
est kind."

From the North Star.

" After waiting several weeks, we have received a copy of this
little work. It is certainly one of the most interesting and
thrilling narratives of slavery ever laid before the American
people. The exposure which the author makes of the horrors
of slavery—the separations—the whippings, and the accumulated
outrages inflicted on the slave, must stir the blood of every
reader who has the pulsations of a man. The description of the

slave's longing for freedom—of his deception, tricks and stratagems to escape his condition, is just, though humiliating. His
narrations of the cruelty of individual slaveholders, is natural,
and we doubt not in every essential particular is true. We
deem the work a most valuable acquisition to the anti-slavery
cause ; and we hope that it may be widely circulated through
out the country."

From the Chronotype.

" This fugitive slave literature is destined to be a powerful
lever. We have the most profound conviction of its potency.
We see in it the easy and infallible means of abolitionizing the
free states. Argument provokes argument, reason is met by
sophistry. But narratives of slaves go right to the hearts of
men. We defy any man to think with any patience or tolerance
of slavery after reading Bibb's narrative, unless he is one of
those infidels to nature who float on the race as monsters, from
it, but not of it. Put a dozen copies of this book into every
school district or neighborhood in the Free States- and we
have known candidates of the Free Soil party whose wealth
would not miss the requisite to do it—and you might sweep the
whole north on a thorough going Liberty Platform for abolish-
ing slavery, everywhere and every how. Stir up honest men's
souls with such a book and they won't set much by *disclaimers*,
they won't be squeamish how radically they vote against a system which surpasses any hell which theology has ever been
able to conjure up.
" We believe this to be an unvarnished tale, giving a true
picture of slavery in all its features, good, bad and indifferent,
if it has so many. The book is written with perfect artlessness,
and the man who can read it unmoved must be fit for treasons,
stratagems and spoils.
" One conclusion forced upon the philosophical reader of such
narratives of runaway slaves is this, that however tolerable
chattel slavery may be as an institution for savage and barbarous
life, when you bring it into the purlieus of civilization and
Christianity, it becomes unspeakably iniquitous and intolerable.
If Mr. Calhoun really means to uphold slavery, he *must*—there
is no help for it—abolish Christianity, printing, art, science, and
take his patriarchs back to the standard of Central Africa or the
days of Shem, Ham and Japhet."

INDEX.

INDEX. **211**

APPENDIX

CHRONOLOGY OF HENRY BIBB

BIBLIOGRAPHY

APPENDIX

I. Letter from Henry Bibb to James G. Birney,
25 February 1845

Bibb, like other successful fugitive slave orators, faced challenges to his credibility as a writer. On one hand, he was an eloquent witness against slavery. On the other hand, his very eloquence undermined the notion that he had ever been a slave. Moreover, Bibb's daring return for his family and his repeated escapes probably led some to doubt the details of the episodes he described. Bibb wrote the following letter to James G. Birney, a prominent abolitionist who had some reservations about Bibb's truthfulness. Both Birney's reservations and Bibb's comments refer to the oral narrative that Bibb presented on the antislavery lecture platform in the early 1840s, before the publication of his written *Narrative* in 1849. In the letter Bibb asserts his continuing concern for his wife and child and anticipates the gathering of materials by the Detroit Liberty Party Committee later in 1845. Bibb used some of those documents as his prefatory authentication four years later when he published his *Narrative.*

In his written *Narrative,* Bibb notes that he had only a few weeks of schooling in Detroit, and in the preface to his *Narrative* he apologizes for his lack of facility with English grammar. This unedited letter indicates that Lucius Matlack's role as editor was largely in terms of proofreading and standardizing Bibb's spelling. It also supports C. Peter Ripley's contention that Mary E. Miles Bibb was instrumental in preparing the *Voice of the Fugitive* for publication.

DETROIT FEBY 25TH 1845

Esteem Friend

After my respects to you. Sir I thank you very kindly for your remarks respecting my Narative. you suposed that I was an imposter & was kind a neugh to tell me for my own good. I had better go home & go to work & that I must stop or you would expose me & & I have offten wished that I could find a friend of high standing who would tell my very kindly & plain what he thought of my story after hearing my Lectures. but you are the only gentleman that have spoken so frankly on the subject. —it is tru I have not been as carful in explaining dates and some other things as I should have been which has led you & others to doubt my honesty. but I am now trying to colect some facts to prove the reality of my Narative & by so doing I hope to be able to prove to the public that I am honest in pleeding the cause of a poor broken hearted wife & child, who ware severd from my imbrace by a professor of Religion & they are now clanking thir Chanes in slavery. Oh when I think of it My heart birns with endegnation against slavery. yeas, when I think of that wife & child who was dearer than Life haveing to take the parting hand never to meet againe in this Life with bursting crys of sorrow flung from hert to hert & souding in my year & at the same time a profest Christen could put the lash on. These things help to make me a strong Abolitionist. am I not Justifiable in exposeing such Christianity. have I not a rite to pleed my own cause & the cause of the enslaved, being responsible. Sir nothing but for want of ability shall ever prevent me from a faithful discharge of my duty to my enslaved Cuntryman. I Close by saying I am a friend to my Cuntry & to all who are oppresst & all tho I may be denounced & calld

an imposter, because I am of the dispised Race yet I hop I shall be able to prove to the world that I have told the truth & I will be herd for my people.
Truly yours,

Henry Bibb and
Liberty forever

II. Prospectus of the *Voice of the Fugitive*

The Prospectus for the *Voice of the Fugitive* clearly indicates Bibb's antislavery ideals and solicits support from like-minded subscribers and contributors. Bibb's continued emphasis on the separation of families as a characteristic of slavery is notable. Even though the banner for the paper reads *Voice of the Fugitive,* the prospectus refers to "Voice of the Fugitives."

VOICE OF THE FUGITIVE 1 JANUARY 1851
Prospectus
Voice of the Fugitives
(In Canada),
is to be the title of a Newspaper published by
Mr. Henry Bibb,
At Sandwich, Canada West, Near Detroit Michigan

It is designed to be an organ through which the refugees from Southern Slavery may be heard both in America and Europe. The first copy will be issued in January, 1851, on a medium sized sheet, and will be published but twice a month, until we shall obtain a sufficient number of subscribers to support a weekly.

To do this, and to spread out our cause widely before the world, we would most respectfully solicit all to whom this may come—and especially such as are interested in the elevation of those of us who, after many long years of unrequited toil, have succeeded, by the help of God, in making our way to where we may glorify Him with our bodies and spirits, which are His—to subscribe for the paper. And if any should wish to know whether Fugitives can take care of themselves, after becoming free of bondage, subscribe for the paper. If any wish to know how we enjoy liberty, and what we think of those who robbed us of our wives, children, and all that is sacred and dear, let them subscribe for the paper. If you would like to give utterance to the dumb by aiding us in proclaiming liberty to captives, and the opening of the prison to those that are bound, contribute and subscribe for the paper!

The terms will be One Dollar a year, to be paid always in advance.

Will those who are interested in the success of our enterprise give us a lift in the start? Will you act as agents, and forward to us before the 1st of January next? Only make us to feel that we shall be backed up by anti-slavery sympathy, and we shall go forward with strength and courage.

All letters from the United States must be directed to Detroit, Michigan, and those from Canada and England, to Sandwich.

III. Henry Bibb's Statement of Editorial Policy, from the first issue of *Voice of the Fugitive*, 1 January 1851

In the first issue of the *Voice of the Fugitive,* Bibb stated the issues, which consumed the remainder of his career: abolition, emigration, religion, education, temperance, and moral reform.

VOICE OF THE FUGITIVE 1 JANUARY 1851
Introduction

In introducing the Voice of the Fugitives to its patrons, the rules of propriety, as well as a long established custom, make it our duty to set forth some avowal of the principles by which we shall be governed in its editorial management. In doing this, we wish to be honest to ourselves and to our readers. We make no flattering promises in advance, knowing that we shall be judged by our works as they shall appear.

To make a competent editor, we are not unmindful of the fact, that there are several qualifications which are necessary. He must be a man of talent, a ready writer, with prudence and literary attainments, well seasoned with good common sense. But we do not claim for ourselves but a very limited degree of either; therefore, it is pressing necessity alone that has impelled us to the task.

We expect, by the aid of a good Providence, to advocate the cause of human liberty in the true meaning of that term. We shall advocate the immediate and unconditional abolition of chattel slavery every where, but especially on the American soil. We shall also persuade, as far as it may be practicable, every oppressed person of color in the United States to settle in Canada, where the laws make no distinction among men, based on complection, and upon whose soil "no slave can breathe." We shall advocate the claims of the American slaves to the Bible, from whom it has ever been withheld. We shall advocate the cause of Temperance and moral reform generally. The cause of education shall have a prominent space in our columns. We shall advocate the claims of agricultural pursuits among our people, as being the most certain road to independence and self-respect.

Our political creed shall be to support that Government that protects all men in the enjoyment of Liberty, without regard to color. We shall oppose the annexation of Canada to the United States to the fullest extent of our ability, while that Government continues to tolerate the abominable system of human slavery.

We shall from time to time endeavor to lay before our readers the true condition of our people in Canada, of their hopes and prospects for the future—and while we intend this to be a mouth piece for refugees in Canada especially, yet we mean to speak out our sentiments as a FREEMAN upon all subjects that come within our sphere; and if others differ with us, as they probably will, on some subjects, all we shall ask will be the toleration of opinion and free discussion, which is the refutation of error and the bulwark of liberty. We shall make no compromise with wrong, nor allow personal controversies in our paper. But any thing written in respectful language, by way of reply or explanation shall always have attention, but we must be the judge of what is suitable to go into our columns.

IV. Henry Bibb Editorial on Education from *Voice of the Fugitive* 15 January 1851

The following editorial shows the continuing importance of literacy for Bibb and in his view, the development of the African American community. Note Bibb's ongoing emphasis on the separation of families as a major horror of slavery.

VOICE OF THE FUGITIVE 15 JANUARY 1851
Education

We regard the education of colored people in North America as being one of the most important measures connected with the destiny of our race. By it we can be strengthened and elevated—without it we shall be ignorant, weak, and degraded. By it we shall be clothed with a power which will enable us to arise from degradation and command respect from the whole civilized world: without it we shall ever be imposed upon, oppressed and enslaved; not that we are more stupid than others would be under the same circumstances, indeed very few races of men have the corporal ability to survive, under the same physical and mental depression that the colored race have to endure, and still retain their manhood.

In most of the slave States where the colored people are compelled to work under the slave-driver's lash, without wages, they are often sold apart from their families, handcuffed and branded with hot irons, and forbid by statute law to read the name of God. Under such treatment, almost any other race would have sunk in despair.

Show us a community of white people, even in a free country, where they may possess all the natural advantages of climate and soil that the world was ever blessed with, and let there be no schools, no post-offices, no newspapers circulated or read, no mental instruction given, orally or otherwise, and we could write out the character of that people. They would have a grog-shop at almost every public place; they would be ignorant, vicious, and licentious; the county jails would seldom be unoccupied by prisoners, the courts would be continually annoyed by petty lawsuits, and the county heavily taxed for the support of paupers.

With this mass of degradation before us, we say that the most effectual remedy for the above evils is education. It is the best fortune that a father can give his son; it is a treasure that can never be squandered, and one that will always command respect and secure a good livelihood for an industrious person.

But we speak now especially to our fugitive brethren. We frequently hear persons say that they are too far advanced in life to learn to read and write. To all such we say, be not discouraged. We think there are but very few who could not be taught to read the Bible, if they would only commence and persevere. If we learn to read that, we can then learn to read other books and papers, and we should understand the laws of Government under which we live. To do this we should read, in order to become wise, intelligent, and useful in society. We should at least know how to read and write; and when we have learned this, we have the best means with which to educate ourselves.

V. Mary E. Bibb Editorial on Schools from 26 February 1851 *Voice of the Fugitive*

This editorial was written and signed by Bibb's second wife, Mary E. Miles Bibb. It clearly indicates her zeal for education and points out some of the problems in starting an educational program in the fugitive community.

VOICE OF THE FUGITIVE 26 FEBRUARY 1851
Schools

No doubt it will be interesting to many to hear something respecting schools in this part of the province. The day school in this place has increased from twelve to forty-six, notwithstanding the embarrassing circumstances under which it started, namely, a dark ill-ventilated room, uncomfortable seats, want of desks, books and all sorts of school apparatus. I would mention with gratitude the assistance from friends in Lenewee county, Michigan, through the agency of J. F. Dolbear, which enabled me to procure a black board and the few books with which we commenced. He has the united thanks of all connected with the school for his timely visit; many of whom, six weeks ago, could not tell one letter from another, can now spell intelligibly in Town's Spelling-book, and read any of the exercises contained therein. This may seem strange to many, but not to one at all acquainted with physiology. It is an accredited fact that persons whose physical system is well developed, learn much faster than those whose mental capacities are over-taxed at an earlier age.

The Learned Blacksmith is regarded as the wonder of the age. Truly, he is a hero! What shall we say of men, and *women too,* who have spent a life in slavery, enduring the separation of loved ones, who, having escaped to the nominally free States, in pursuit of freedom, found a prejudice equally withering. Overcoming all this, and feeling that they were men among men, standing upon free soil, awoke only to hear the sound of Mason's infamous fugitive bill.

What shall we say of those who have again taken their lives in their hands and escaped to this desolate, cold country, where they are again strangers in a strange land, who, having endured all this, together with the cares of a family on the one hand and pressing want on the other? Is not the person who can improve under such circumstances a hero, even according to Thomas Carlyle's own showing? Many of these support themselves by their own industry, improving all their time to good advantage.

Are such persons worthy? Is it not doing good to help such to possess so great a treasure as education? The friends in the States would render these people a great good by turning their attention more to schools. To do anything the teachers should be such as know what material they have to operate upon; and, knowing this, they should have something wherewith to work—the sympathy of friends and an assurance of being sustained—otherwise there cannot be good schools in Canada.

We acknowledge with gratitude the books presented by Mr. Cook, of Adrian, who is a young man, and has done much for Canada mission. They certainly were a God-send.

We commenced a Sunday-school four weeks ago; present, thirty-six; there are now forty-four members, and much interest is manifested both by parents and children, some coming even in inclement weather the distance of two and three miles. We are entirely destitute of bibles, there being but four testaments in the school, one of these being minus several chapters.

Mr. Coe, of _____, brought 100 volumes of the Sunday-school library, of these I put into the hands of Coleman Freeman fifty volumes for the Windsor Sabbath school. Many of these scholars commit whole chapters to memory every week.

M. E. BIBB.

VI. Henry Bibb Editorial on Color-Phobia in Canada
from 21 May 1851 *Voice of the Fugitive*

While many slave narratives present the North as an ideal of racial harmony—especially when compared to the South—by 1850, when a stronger fugitive slave law was passed, many blacks moved further north to Canada for the greater safety offered by British rule. In this editorial, however, Bibb indicates that even when the number of blacks increased in Canada, there were problems with color prejudice. Bibb treats this prejudice with a large dose of sarcasm and scorn.

VOICE OF THE FUGITIVE 21 MAY 1851
Color-Phobia in Canada

This most obnoxious and fatal disease has made its way into this province where it is destined to make havoc among the ignorant and vicious if a speedy remedy is not applied. Its allies are mostly among the lowest class of white people, who are used as mere stepping stones or political hobbies for the more refined and enlightened to ride into office upon. Its origin sprang from old Capt. *Slavery,* who has enlisted thousands in his services to carry on the work of prejudice, malice, and hatred, death and devastation among the human family. He has ever been opposed to the spread of knowledge among the common people. The rum shop is substituted for the school house and his soldiers are mostly men [of] intemperate habits; always ready to go at the bidding of their leader to break up an anti-slavery meeting, to engage in the work of kidnapping, man stealing, breaking up the bands of human affections by selling children from parents and husbands from their wives.

In thousands of instances he has enlisted the press and the pulpit in his services, and especially in the U.S. He has secured the Executive and Legislative power of that Government in passing and enforcing the fugitive slave law which is regarded as a disgrace to the christian world.

But the old deceiver is not satisfied with what has been accomplished in the states; but is now striving to get a foot-hold in Canada where many of the objects of his prey have settled under the protection of Her Majesty's law.

Color-phobia is a contagious disease. It is more destructive to the mind than to the body. It goes hard with a person who is a little nervous. It makes them both froth and foam as if the Bengal Tiger was in them. Its symptoms are various. It makes them sing out "darkey," "darkey," "nigger"—sometimes "long-heel"—"long-heel." It sometimes makes them quack like crows. It frightens them up from the dining table at public houses, not because of a black man's cooking the dinner or waiting on the table, but because of his sitting down to eat. It excites them awfully when colored passengers enter the rail cars or stage coaches, but not when they come in the capacity of waiters and servants.

It sometimes gets into children through the wicked and unnatural teaching of parents.—Whenever you hear a parent saying to a child "hush and go to sleep, or the nigger will catch you"—the black man will kill you, &c. It is pretty good evidence that they have got the color-phobia. When they have it bad they will turn up their noses when they get near a colored person, as if they smelt something disagreeable and often say there is a cloud rising. It sometimes gets holds of professors of religion, and shows itself at the communion table, especially if a colored sister offers to partake of the emblems of the dying Saviour with her white brethren—she is modestly asked by one of the Deacons or class leaders to wait until the white folks are done and she is seated up in the back corner of the gallery or in the back part of the house (perhaps under the steps).

In Canada, it gets hold of the very dregs of society. It makes them shudder at the idea of "negro settlement" "they will ruin the country" &c. The objection most generally brought up is that we shall have negro lawyers, doctors, judges &c. It seems to excite their imagination so much that they become alarmed about amalgamation—the white girls are all going to make choice of black men, and the white gents will be left without wives, and what then? Don't be alarmed friends, you shall not be hurt. All this is the workings of a diseased imagination, of which you must be cured, or it will destroy your souls and bodies both. Anti-Slavery is the very best remedy for it. It will cure you of prejudice and hatred, and prepare you for a happier state of existence.

VII. Henry Bibb Editorial on The American Refugees Home from 18 June 1851 *Voice of the Fugitive*

After the passage of a stronger fugitive slave law in 1850 and his own immigration to Canada, Bibb became a major advocate of Canadian immigration for American blacks. Bibb and his wife were major proponents of the American Refugees Home. This editorial gives a sense of the conditions and the somewhat utopian ideal that Bibb and others worked toward in attempting to establish this community.

VOICE OF THE FUGITIVE 18 JUNE 1851
The American Refugees Home

To the friends of civil liberty and education, we would most respectfully represent that the number of human beings held in chattel slavery in the U. States is over and above 3,000,000; and that they are not only prohibited in several of the slave States by statute law from reading, the scriptures of Divine Truth as a means of grace—but the most sacred ties of the human family are frequently and wickedly broken up by selling husbands from wives and children from parents. From such oppression as this, people are constantly running away to the North, and thousands of whom have been compelled to take refuge in Canada under the British flag, which protects them in the enjoyment of that liberty which the American Government has so earnestly sought to take from unoffending people.

It is not now our purpose, however, to enlarge upon the evils of that system "one hour of which is fraught with far greater misery than ages of that which" the fathers of the

American Republic, "rose in rebellion to oppose," for we presume there are none who will read this circular but what will admit its intrinsic sinfulness. But our object is simply to lay facts before the public, relative to the rapid influx and actual condition of our refugee brethren in Canada since the enactment of the notorious Fugitive Slave Law in the U.S., and to arrive at, if possible, what kind of assistance would result in the most permanent good to the greatest number of this people who are now in Canada and who may hereafter come.

It was generally supposed before the passage of the fugitive slave law that there were from 25 to 35 thousand who had taken refuge here, and since that enactment the number has greatly augmented—from the fact that it is now well understood that there is no protection to the liberty of a refugee slave in America, until the Canadian line is drawn between him and his pursuer.

The sad story of the fugitives *Long, Syms, Wordman* and a host of others who have been dragged back into perpetual slavery by the strong arm of the American government, furnishes sufficient proof of the truthfulness of this assertion.

The condition of this people in Canada, as a general thing, is that they are here in a strange land from necessity, uneducated, poverty stricken, without homes or any permanent means of self support; however willing they may be to work they have no means to work with or land to work upon. The natural inference is that they must either beg, starve or steal. To prevent this much has been sent to Canada during the last 7 months by the friends of humanity, in the way of food and clothing for the fugitives. But such help is only temporary and must be repeated again and again, while it is degrading to some extent to all who are recipients thereof—for no people can be respected who live beneath the dignity of manhood. Ignorance, dissipation and pauperism are the landmarks of slavery, and the great aim and object, therefore, should be to enable this people to arise above it by their own industry. The remedy for the physical wants of this people, those especially specified, lies slumbering in the virgin soil of C[anada]. W[est]. To improve the moral, mental and political condition of a poverty stricken and degraded people, they must become owners and tillers of the soil— and PRODUCE WHAT THEY CONSUME.

It is no exaggeration for us to say that more than two-thirds of the refugees in Canada understand agricultural labor and would follow it for a livelihood, had they land or the means to purchase it. They would also gladly open schools for their children that they might be educated for usefulness in life, had they the means with which to do it.

Without homes or employment they are poorly qualified to produce the necessaries of life, to educate the youth or extend the hospitable hand to the gradual emigration of other fugitives who are constantly arriving here, who go up and down these shores hunting shelter and employment but finding none. In order that there may be a permanent asylum to conduct such persons to on the Queen's soil, where the cause of education, industry and morality may be promoted, the friends of humanity in Michigan have organized a state society for the purpose of making an "effort at home and abroad" to purchase 50,000 acres of Canada land for this object, and they propose to deed to the family of every actual settler 5 acres of said land and to leave adjoining it 20 acres which may be purchased by said settler at cost and that one-third of all money paid in for said land by settlers should be appropriated for the support of schools for their children, and that the balance should be kept at interest in the bank for the purchase of more land for the same object from time to time while slavery exists in the United States.

The undersigned being a resident of Canada, has been solicited to write a circular embracing such facts as might be necessary to throw light upon the subject; but for want of time we have not been able to give the subject that consideration which its overwhelming importance demands.

In conclusion we would remark that the Canada Company offer 700,000 acres of land in blocks containing from 2000 to 9000 acres each, situated in the Western District, and scattered lots containing from 100 to 200 acres each, situated in almost every township in Canada West.

The above land is located in the most *southern and western* part of Canada, and is selling from $2 to $4 per acre.

The land is rich and generally well stocked with valuable timber. It is surrounded on either side with lasting and navigable waters. The climate is as mild and congenial to the physical and intellectual development of the African race as a part of Missouri, Ohio, Michigan, Wisconsin or New York; and the argument which is frequently brought up by pro-slavery men that it is so cold that colored people cannot live here is a falsehood and the facts in the case will prove it to be so, from the fact there are at the present time some thirty-five thousand living here who generally arrive at as old an age as they do in the south, and from the fact that when negro slavery was tolerated and practiced here under the colonial government that there was no complaint about the climate's being too cold for the colored people then, affords the most striking proof to our mind that wherever a white man can live and prosper that a colored man can also, if he is given an equal chance. There will always be objections enough brought up against any scheme to settle the colored people this side of Liberia, by prejudiced pro-slavery men. But we say to the true friends of the refugees in Canada, that there never was a time when they could have conferred a more permanent blessing upon this people than to enable them now to purchase some of this land to settle upon.

H. BIBB

VIII and IX. Henry Bibb Public Letter to Albert G. Sibley, "A Letter to my Old Master" from 23 September and 7 October 1852 *Voice of the Fugitive*

In his years as an antislavery speaker prior to the publication of his *Narrative,* Bibb had participated in the antislavery convention of writing a public letter to rebuke his former master. Bibb included his recollection of one of these letters in his *Narrative.* In 1852 he wrote several new letters to Albert G. Sibley, who, through marriage to Harriet White, owned Bibb until 1836 when he sold him to his brother John Sibley. Note how Bibb rhetorically plays on their brotherhood and fellowship in the Methodist Episcopal Church.

VOICE OF THE FUGITIVE 23 SEPTEMBER 1852
A Letter to My Old Master

Mr. Albert G. Sibley:
Sir,
It has now been about sixteen years since we saw each other face to face, and at which time you doubtless considered me inferior to yourself, as you then held me as an article of property, and sold me as such; but my mind soon after became insubordinate to the ungodly relation of master and slave; and the work of self-emancipation commenced and I was made free.

I have long felt inclined to open a correspondence with you upon this subject, but have refrained from doing so, until now, for two reasons; first, I knew not your post office address; and secondly, you then held in bondage several of my mother's children, of which you robbed her when you left the State of Kentucky in 1836. But as those obstacles are now both removed out of the way, I can venture to address you.

For more than twenty years you have been a member of the Methodist Episcopal Church—a class-leader and an exhorter of that denomination; professing to take the *Bible,* as your standard of christian duty. But sir know ye not that in the light of this book, you have been acting the hypocrite all this while? I feel called upon as a christian to call your attention to a few facts with regard to it. But before doing so, I am happy to inform you that my brothers, John, Lewis, and Granville, whose legs brought them from your plantation, are now all at my house in Canada, with our dear mother, free and doing well on British soil: so you need not give yourself any trouble about advertising or looking for them. They have all served you as slaves for 21 to 30 years without compensation, and have now commenced to act for themselves. Is this compatible with the character of a Bible christian? And yet I suppose that you, with your man robbing posse have chased them with your dogs and guns, as if they were sheep-killing wolves upon the huge mountain's brow, for the purpose of re-capturing and dragging them back to a mental graveyard, in the name of law and slaveholding religion. Oh! what harmony there seems to be between those two twin sisters; the Fugitive Slave Law and the Methodist E. Church. Listen to the language of inspiration: "Feed the hungry, and clothe the naked:" "Break every yoke and let the *oppressed go free:*" All things, whatsoever ye would that men should do unto you, do ye even so unto them, for *this is* the law and the prophets."

While on the other hand your church sanctions the buying and selling of men, women, and children: the robbing men of their wives, and parents of their offspring—the violation of the whole of the decalogue, by permitting the profanation of the sabbath; committing of theft, murder, incest and adultery, which is constantly done by church members holding slaves and form the very essence of slavery. Now Sir, allow me with the greatest deference to your intelligence to inform you that you are miserably deceiving yourself, if you believe that you are in the straight and narrow path to heaven, whilst you are practising such abominable violations of the plainest precepts of religion.

The fellowship of no number of professing christians, however extended nor the solemn baptism and silent toleration of all the Reverend time serving ministers in creation, can make you really a christian, or dispense with the binding force of the Gospel of Jesus Christ, as the rule of your life and practice; and whilst you continue in such an unhallowed course of conduct, your prayers and your solemn fasts and ordinances are an abomination to the Lord from which he will turn his face away, in disgust, and will not hear or look upon.

I must here conclude for the present, but as this subject is fraught with such vital importance to your eternal interest and as I have once maintained an intimate relation to you, I shall feel bound as a christian to interest myself in calling your attention to it again.

Yours with becoming respect,

HENRY BIBB

WINDSOR SEPT. 23 1852

VOICE OF THE FUGITIVE 7 OCTOBER 1852
Letter to My Old Master, No. 2

Mr. Albert G. Sibley:
Sir,
At the close of my last I promised to call your attention to this subject again—and in doing so my object is not

merely to convince you that I have acquired the art of communicating my thoughts intelligibly on paper to be read by tyrants, notwithstanding they with yourself have done their best to keep me in perpetual bondage and ignorance—but it is to warn you of the great danger to which you are exposed while standing in the attitude of an incorrigible slaveholder. I mean that you shall know that there is a just God in heaven, who cannot harmonise human slavery with the Christian religion: I mean that you know there is a law which is more binding upon the consciences of slaves than that of Congress, or any other human enactment—and I mean that you shall know that all of your slaves have escaped to Canada, where they are just as free as yourself, and that we have not forgotten the cruel treatment which we received at your hands while in the state of slavery. I have often heard you say that a slave who was well fed, and clothed, was far better off than a "free Negro," who had no master to provide for and take care of him.

Now with all candour in answer to this proslavery logic, let me ask who is it that takes care of the slaveholders and their families? Who is it that clears up the forest, cultivates the Land, manages the stock, husbands the grain, and prepares it for table? Who is it that digs from the cotton, sugar, and rice fields the means with which to build southern Cities, Steam boats, School houses and churches? I answer that it is the slaves, that perform this labor, and yet they or their children are not permitted to enjoy any of the benefits of these Institutions: our former slaves who are now British subjects, are about trying the *dangerous experiment* of taking care of themselves—which has so far proved to be a very successful one. Their services are worth to them here upon an average one dollar per day—

they are also attending a night School for the purpose of learning to read and write. With the above facts before me, I am led to the conclusion that the slave who can take care of himself and master both can certainly take care of himself alone, if he is only given a fair chance. Oh! tell me not then Sir, that a man is happier and better off in a state of chattel bondage than in a state of freedom. The idea of a man being a slave—of being subjected to the will and power of a master, is revolting to his very nature. Freedom for ones-self though poorly clad, and fed with a dry crust, is glorious when compared with American slavery, even if it should, appear dressed in broad cloth, and fed with all of the luxuries which the human appetite could desire. This right is highly appreciated by the wild beasts of the forest and the fowls of the air. The terrific screech of the hooting owl is animating to himself and musical to his kind as he goes through the tall forest, from the hill top, to the valley. Not so, with the miserable little screech owl, while he is tied by the leg or boxed up in a cage though well fed he is made the sport of children. The startling scream of the wild panther, or the roar of the lion—it is majestic and independent in their native desert. Not so when they are chained in a cage to be fed by a "kind master," on Johnny cake, roast beef, or no beef just as he chooses. But my illustrations are inadequate to describe the injustice, and my abhorrence of slaveholding.

Again I call your attention to the moral bearing of this subject, as it applies to yourself. You profess to be a christian [*sic*]—a leader in the M. E. Church, and a representative of the Lord Jesus Christ, and yet you sold my mother from her little children, and sent them away to a distant land—you sold my brother George from his wife and dear little ones, while he was a worthy member, and Clergyman, of the same Church, to which *you belong.* In early life you also compelled me to cheat, lie and *steal* from your neighbours. You have often made me drive up sheep, and hogs, which you knew to be the property of your neighbors and slaughter them for market and the use of your own table.

The language of Holy writ is that "thou shalt not steal," "let every man have his own wife, and every woman her own husband," and parents are strictly required to train up their children in the fear and admonition of the Lord. Every one of these Holy injunctions you have wickedly, and willingly broken. Oh! what hypocrisy is this? A Methodist class leader, selling a Methodist Minister—a Methodist class leader separating husbands and wives—a Methodist class leader, stealing and slaughtering his neighbors sheep and hogs. Vain is your religion—base is your hypocrisy. We have no confidence in your sheep stealing, and man robbing religion. My brothers, Granville, John, and Lewis, all unite in corroborating the above facts: and if you dare to deny a single word of it let us hear from you and we will furnish undoubted proof.

Yours with due respect,

H. BIBB

P.S. If you do not answer this soon you may expect to hear from me again.

CHRONOLOGY OF HENRY BIBB

1815

May

Henry Bibb, also known as Walton H. Bibb, is born in Shelby County, Kentucky, to Milldred Jackson, a slave, and James Bibb, a white male. Bibb is the eldest of Jackson's seven sons. Bibb is born the slave of David White, Esq.

1825

Bibb begins his first efforts at short-term running away, or maroonage.

1833

Bibb visits conjurers to escape punishment for staying out too late and for love potions.

Bibb meets and falls in love with Malinda.

Bibb enters into a "conditional contract of matrimony [with Malinda], viz: that we would marry if our minds should not change within one year." (37)

1834

December

Bibb marries Malinda.

1835

When his owner, Albert Sibley, decides to move to Missouri, Bibb is sold to John Sibley, who lives within seven miles of Malinda's owner.

John Sibley sells Bibb to Malinda's owner, William Gatewood.

1835?

The Bibbs' daughter Mary Frances is born.

1837

25 December

Bibb makes his first escape to the North.

1838

May

Bibb returns to Kentucky in an attempt to rescue his family.

June

Bibb returns to Cincinnati and waits for Malinda and Mary Frances to join him. Bibb is captured in Cincinnati and returned as far as Louisville, where he escapes again. Bibb returns to the Gatewood plantation to rescue his family.

Fall

Bibb returns to Ohio and waits for Malinda and Mary Frances to join him.

1839

July

Bibb returns to Kentucky to rescue his family. Bibb is betrayed and captured; he and his family are sold and transported to Louisiana after spending several months in the Louisville jail.

Fall

Bibb and his family are sold to Deacon Whitfield, who has a plantation in the Red River area of Louisiana.

1840

December

Bibb is sold to a group of traveling gamblers as punishment after two failed attempts to run away from Whitfield.

1841

The gamblers sell Bibb to a Native American in the Arkansas Indian Territory.

Spring

Bibb escapes to the North when his owner dies.

Bibb begins telling his oral narrative from the anti-slavery platform.

Bibb receives three weeks of schooling in Detroit with W. C. Monroe.

1843

Bibb attends a convention of free blacks in Detroit.

1844

23 March

Bibb writes a letter to his former owner, William Gatewood, explaining his flight from slavery.

1844–1845

Bibb campaigns for the Liberty Party ticket in Michigan and Ohio.

1845

25 February

Bibb writes a letter to James G. Birney noting his attempts to gather authenticating documents and emphasizing his desire to reunite his slave family.

22 April

The Liberty Party committee in Detroit gathers authenticating material and issues a report on the credibility of Bibb and the events he recounts.

Bibb is employed fulltime as an antislavery lecturer.

Winter

Bibb goes to Madison, Indiana, to get news from Kentucky. He claims that he learns his wife, Malinda, has been her owner's paramour for the past three years.

1847

May

Bibb meets and begins a courtship of Mary E. Miles.

1848

June

Bibb marries Mary E. Miles.
Bibb attends the founding meeting of the Free Soil
Party along with Frederick Douglass, Samuel R.
Ward, Henry Highland Garnet, and Lewis Clark.

1849

*Narrative of the Life and Adventures of Henry Bibb,
An American Slave; Written by Himself* is published.

1 July

Lucius Matlack's introduction to the *Narrative* is
signed and dated.

1850

Bibb's *Narrative* enters its third edition.
Bibb and his wife, Mary, emigrate to Chatham,
Canada West. The Bibbs become advocates of
abolition, emigration, agricultural enterprise for
fugitive slaves in Canada.

1851

1 January

Bibb becomes editor and publisher of the bi-
monthly *Voice of the Fugitive,* the first black
newspaper in Canada. The paper is published in
Sandwich, Canada West.

Fall

Bibb encourages and promotes a black emigration
convention in Toronto.

9 September

At the Toronto emigration convention Bibb advocates separatism and independence based on agriculture, views which he also promotes in the *Voice
of the Fugitive.*

January 1851–October 1853

The Bibbs found a day school for fugitive slaves. The Bibbs help to build a Methodist Church. The Bibbs are active in antislavery and temperance work and in a society to greet and aid fugitive slaves from the United States.

1852

The *Voice of the Fugitive* has agents in Michigan, Ohio, Pennsylvania, New York, and New Hampshire; Martin Delany is the agent in Pittsburgh. Bibb claims 1100 subscribers for the first year of publication. Editorially, Bibb advocates agriculture as the "most certain road to independence and self-respect," defends blacks against attacks by white Canadian racists, and promotes emigration to Canada.

June

James Theodore Holly becomes co-editor and co-proprietor of the *Voice of the Fugitive.*

23 September, 7 October

Bibb publishes a series of public letters to Albert Sibley, one of his former owners.

December

Bibb announces the paper will be renamed "Voice of the Fugitive and Canadian Independent."

1853

March

Provincial Freeman, the second black newspaper in Canada, begins competing with Bibb; Samuel Ringgold Ward is the titular editor but the paper is actually operated by Mary Ann Shadd Cary. The two papers attack each other in terms of assimilation versus separatism, permanent emigration in

Canada versus temporary residence, and anti-begging versus solicitation of funds to support the fugitives.

October

Bibb's printing office is destroyed by a fire, which Bibb believes was arson.

1854

1 August

Bibb dies in Canada at the age of thirty-nine.

BIBLIOGRAPHY

Andrews, William L. "The Changing Rhetoric of the Nineteenth-Century Slave Narrative of the United States." In *Slavery in the Americas*, ed. Wolfgang Binder, 471–86. Würzburg, Germany: Königshausen und Neumann, 1993.

Andrews, William L. "Dialogue in Ante-bellum Afro-American Autobiography." In *Studies in Autobiography*, ed. James Olney, 89–98. New York: Oxford University Press, 1988.

Andrews, William L. "The 1850s: The First Afro-American Renaissance." In *Literary Romanticism in America*, 38–60. Baton Rouge: Louisiana State University Press, 1981.

Andrews, William L. Introduction to *Three Classic African-American Novels*, 7–21. New York: Mentor, 1990.

Andrews, William L. "The Novelization of Voice in Early African American Narrative." *Publications of the Modern Language Association* 105 (1990): 23–34.

Andrews, William L. *To Tell a Free Story: The First Century of Afro-American Autobiography, 1760–1865.* Urbana: University of Illinois Press, 1988.

Barthes, Roland. "An Introduction to the Structural Analysis of Narrative." *New Literary History* 6 (1975): 237–72.

Bayliss, John F. Introduction to *Black Slave Narratives*, 7–21. New York: Macmillan, 1970.

Bell, Bernard W. *The Afro-American Novel and Its Tradition.* Amherst: University of Massachusetts Press, 1987.

Bell, Bernard W. "Literary Sources of the Early Afro-

American Novel." *College Language Association Journal* 18 (1974): 29–43.

Bentley, Nancy. "White Slaves: The Mulatto Hero in Antebellum Fiction." *American Literature* 65 (1993): 501–22.

Bibb, Henry. "Henry Bibb to Birney; 25 February 1845." In *Letters of James Gillespie Birney, 1831–1857*. Vol. 2, ed. Dwight L. Dumond, 928. Gloucester, Mass.: Peter Smith, 1966.

Bibb, Henry. "Henry Bibb to the Executive Committee of the American Missionary Association; 14 December 1850, 14 April 1851." In *The Black Abolitionist Papers*. Vol. 2, ed. C. Peter Ripley et al., 113–18. Chapel Hill: University of North Carolina Press, 1986.

Bibb, Henry. *Narrative of the Life and Adventures of Henry Bibb, an American Slave; Written by Himself*. 3rd Stereotype ed. New York: n. p., 1850.

Blassingame, John W. Introduction to *Slave Testimony: Two Centuries of Letters, Speeches, Interviews, and Autobiographies*, xvii–lxv. Baton Rouge: Louisiana State University Press, 1977.

Blassingame, John W. *The Slave Community: Plantation Life in the Ante-bellum South*. New York: Oxford University Press, 1972.

Bontemps, Arna. *Great Slave Narratives*. Boston: Beacon, 1969.

Braxton, Joanne M. *Black Women Writing Autobiography: A Tradition within a Tradition*. Philadelphia: Temple University Press, 1989.

Brignano, Russell. *Black Americans in Autobiography*. Westport, Conn.: Greenwood, 1972.

Brown, Sterling. *The Negro in American Fiction*. 1937. Port Washington, N.Y.: Kennikat Press, 1968.

Brown, William Wells. *Clotel, or, The President's Daughter: A Narrative of Slave Life in the United States; With a Sketch of the Author's Life.* 1853. In *Three Classic African-American Novels*, ed. William L. Andrews, 71–283. New York: Mentor, 1990.

Brown, William Wells. *Narrative of William W. Brown, A Fugitive Slave; Written by Himself.* 1847. In *From Fugitive Slave to Free Man: The Autobiographies of William Wells Brown*, ed. William L. Andrews, 15–109. New York: Mentor, 1993.

Butterfield, Stephen. *Black Autobiography in America.* Amherst: University of Massachusetts Press, 1974.

Carby, Hazel V. *Reconstructing Womanhood: The Emergence of the Afro-American Woman Novelist.* New York: Oxford University Press, 1987.

Davis, Charles T. "The Slave Narrative: First Major Art Form in an Emerging Black Tradition." In *Black Is the Color of the Cosmos: Essays on Afro-American Literature and Culture, 1942–1981*, ed. Henry Louis Gates, Jr., 83–119. New York: Garland, 1982.

Davis, Charles T. and Henry Louis Gates, Jr. "Introduction: The Language of Slavery." In *The Slave's Narrative*, xi–xxxiv. New York: Oxford University Press, 1985.

Delany, Martin R. *Blake, or, The Huts of America.* 1859–62. Ed. Floyd J. Miller. Boston: Beacon, 1970.

Douglas, Ann. *The Feminization of American Culture.* New York: Doubleday, 1987.

Douglass, Frederick. *The Heroic Slave.* 1853. In *Three Classic African-American Novels*, ed. William L. Andrews, 23–69. New York: Mentor, 1990.

Douglass, Frederick. *Life and Times of Frederick Douglass, Written by Himself.* Hartford, Conn.: Park Publishing, 1881.

Douglass, Frederick. *Narrative of the Life of Frederick Douglass, An American Slave; Written by Himself.* 1845. In *The Classic Slave Narratives*, ed. Henry Louis Gates, Jr., 243–331. New York: Mentor, 1987.

Douglass, Frederick. "Shalt Thou Steal?: An Address Delivered in New York, New York, on 8 May 1849." In *The Frederick Douglass Papers: Series One: Speeches, Debates, and Interviews.* Vol. 2., ed. John W. Blassingame, 174–93. New Haven, Conn.: Yale University Press, 1982.

duCille, Ann. *The Coupling Convention: Sex, Text, and Tradition in Black Women's Fiction.* New York: Oxford University Press, 1993.

Dudley, David L. *My Father's Shadow: Intergenerational Conflict in African American Men's Autobiography.* Philadelphia: University of Pennsylvania Press, 1991.

Farrison, William Edward. *William Wells Brown, Author & Reformer.* Chicago: University of Chicago Press, 1969.

Ferguson, Alfred R. "The Abolition of Blacks in Abolitionist Fiction, 1830–1860." *Journal of Black Studies* 5 (1974): 134–56.

Foster, Frances Smith. "'In Respect to Females . . .': Differences in the Portrayals of Women by Male and Female Narrators." *Black American Literature Forum* 15 (1981): 66–70.

Foster, Frances Smith. *Witnessing Slavery: The Development of Ante-bellum Slave Narratives.* Westport, Conn.: Greenwood, 1979.

Foster, Frances Smith. *Written by Herself: Literary Production by African American Women, 1746–1892.* Bloomington: Indiana University Press, 1993.

Franklin, H. Bruce. *The Victim as Criminal and Artist: Literature from the American Prison*. New York: Oxford University Press, 1978.

Gates, Henry Louis, Jr. "Binary Oppositions in Chapter One of *Narrative of the Life of Frederick Douglass an American Slave Written by Himself*." In *Figures in Black: Words, Signs, and the Racial Self*, 80–97. New York: Oxford University Press, 1987.

Gates, Henry Louis, Jr. Introduction to *The Classic Slave Narratives*, ix–xviii. New York: Penguin, 1987.

Genette, Gerard. *Narrative Discourse: An Essay in Method*. Trans. Jane E. Levin. Ithaca, N.Y.: Cornell University Press, 1980.

Gibson, Donald B. "Faith, Doubt, and Apostasy: Evidence of Things Unseen in Frederick Douglass's *Narrative*." In *Frederick Douglass: New Literary and Historical Essays*, ed. Eric J. Sundquist, 84–98. Cambridge: Cambridge University Press, 1990.

Gibson, Donald B. "Reconciling Public and Private in Frederick Douglass' *Narrative*." *American Literature* 57 (1985): 549–69.

Grimes, William. *Life of William Grimes, The Runaway Slave; Written by Himself*. New York: n. p., 1825.

Gutman, Herbert G. *The Black Family in Slavery and Freedom, 1750–1925*. New York: Vintage, 1976.

Hedin, Raymond. "The American Slave Narrative: The Justification of the Picaro." *American Literature* 53 (1982): 630–45.

Hedin, Raymond. "Muffled Voices: The American Slave Narrative." *Clio* 10 (1981): 129–42.

Hedin, Raymond. "Strategies of Form in the American Slave Narrative." In *The Art of the Slave Narrative: Original Essays in Criticism and Theory*, ed. John

Sekora and Darwin T. Turner, 25–35. Macomb: Western Illinois University Press, 1982.

Jackson, Blyden. *A History of Afro-American Literature: The Long Beginning, 1746–1895*. Baton Rouge: Louisiana State University Press, 1989.

Jacobs, Harriet A. [Linda Brent]. *Incidents in the Life of a Slave Girl, Written by Herself*. 1861. Ed. Jean Fagan Yellin. Cambridge, Mass.: Harvard University Press, 1987.

Jones, Howard. "The Peculiar Institution and National Honor: The Case of the *Creole* Slave Revolt." *Civil War History* 21 (1975): 28–50.

Levine, Robert S. *Martin Delaney, Frederick Douglass, and the Politics of Representative Identity*. Chapel Hill: University of North Carolina Press, 1997.

Loggins, Vernon. *The Negro Author: His Development in America*. New York: Columbia University Press, 1931.

McDowell, Deborah E. "In the First Place: Making Frederick Douglass and the Afro-American Narrative Tradition." In *African American Autobiography: A Collection of Critical Essays*, ed. William L. Andrews, 36–58. Englewood Cliffs, N.J.: Prentice Hall, 1993.

McFeely, William S. *Frederick Douglass*. New York: Norton, 1991.

MacKethan, Lucinda H. "From Fugitive Slave to Man of Letters: The Conversion of Frederick Douglass." *The Journal of Narrative Technique* 16 (1986): 55–71.

"Madison Washington: Another Chapter in His History." *Liberator*, 10 June 1842, 89.

Morrison, Toni. *Beloved*. New York: Plume, 1987.

Moses, Wilson J. *Black Messiahs and Uncle Toms: Social*

and Literary Manipulations of a Religious Myth. University Park: Pennsylvania State University Press, 1982.

Nichols, Charles H. *Many Thousand Gone: The Ex-Slaves' Accounts of Their Bondage and Freedom.* Leiden, Netherlands: E.J. Brill, 1963.

Nichols, Charles H. "Who Read the Slave Narratives?" *Phylon* 20 (1959): 149–62.

Niemtzow, Annette. "The Problematic of Self in Autobiography: The Example of the Slave Narrative." In *The Art of the Slave Narrative: Original Essays in Criticism and Theory,* ed. John Sekora and Darwin T. Turner, 96–109. Macomb: Western Illinois University Press, 1982.

Northup, Solomon. *Twelve Years a Slave: Narrative of Solomon Northup, a Citizen of New York, Kidnapped in Washington City in 1841, and Rescued in 1853 from a Cotton Plantation near the Red River in Louisiana.* Ed. David Wilson. Auburn, N.Y.: Derby and Miller, 1853.

Nudelman, Franny. "Harriet Jacobs and the Sentimental Politics of Female Suffering." *English Literary History* 59 (1992): 939–64.

Olney, James. "'I Was Born': Slave Narratives, Their Status as Autobiography and as Literature." In *The Slave's Narrative,* ed. Charles T. Davis and Henry Louis Gates, Jr., 148–75. New York: Oxford University Press, 1985.

Osofsky, Gilbert. "Puttin' on Ole Massa: The Significance of Slave Narratives." In *Puttin' on Ole Massa,* 9–44. New York: Harper, 1969.

Parker, Theodore. "The Position and Duties of the American Scholar." 1849. In *Theodore Parker: American*

Transcendentalist; A Critical Essay and a Collection of His Writings, ed. Robert E. Collins, 103–38. Metuchen, N.J.: Scarecrow, 1973.

Peabody, Ephraim. "Narratives of Fugitive Slaves." In *The Slave's Narrative*, ed. Charles T. Davis and Henry Louis Gates, Jr., 19–28. New York: Oxford University Press, 1985. Originally published in *Christian Examiner,* July–Sep. 1849, 61–93.

Pennington, James W. C. *The Fugitive Blacksmith; or Events in the History of James W. C. Pennington, Pastor of a Presbyterian Church New York, Formerly a Slave in the State of Maryland.* 1849. In *Great Slave Narratives*, ed. Arna Bontemps, 196–267. Boston: Beacon, 1969.

Prince, Gerald. *Narratology: The Form and Functioning of Narrative.* New York: Mouton, 1982.

Rawick, George. *From Sundown to Sunup: The Making of the Black Community.* Westport, Conn.: Greenwood, 1972.

Ripley, C. Peter. Introduction to *The Black Abolitionist Papers.* Vol. 1, ed. Ripley et al., 3–35. Chapel Hill: University of North Carolina Press, 1986.

Ripley, C. Peter. Introduction to *The Black Abolitionist Papers.* Vol. 2, ed. Ripley et al., 2–46. Chapel Hill: University of North Carolina Press, 1986.

Roper, Moses. *A Narrative of the Adventures and Escape of Moses Roper from American Slavery.* Ed. Thomas Price. London: Darton, Harvey and Darton, 1837.

Smith, Sidonie. *Where I'm Bound: Patterns of Slavery and Freedom in Black American Autobiography.* Westport, Conn.: Greenwood, 1974.

Smith, Valerie. *Self-Discovery and Authority in Afro-American Narrative.* Cambridge, Mass.: Harvard University Press, 1987.

Starling, Marion Wilson. *The Slave Narrative: Its Place in American History*. Boston: G.K. Hall, 1982.

Stepto, Robert B. *From behind the Veil: A Study of Afro-American Narrative*. Urbana: University of Illinois Press, 1979.

Stepto, Robert B. "I Rose and Found My Voice: Narration, Authentication, and Authorial Control in Four Slave Narratives." In *The Slave's Narrative*, ed. Charles T. Davis and Henry Louis Gates, Jr., 225–41. New York: Oxford University Press, 1985.

Stepto, Robert B. "Sharing the Thunder: The Literary Exchanges of Harriet Beecher Stowe, Henry Bibb, and Frederick Douglass." In *New Essays on* Uncle Tom's Cabin, ed. Eric J. Sundquist, 135–53. Cambridge: Cambridge University Press, 1986.

Stepto, Robert B. "Storytelling in Early Afro-American Fiction: Frederick Douglass's 'The Heroic Slave.'" In *Black Literature & Literary Theory*, ed. Henry Louis Gates, Jr., 175–86. New York: Routledge, 1990.

Stepto, Robert B. "Teaching Afro-American Literature: Survey or Tradition; The Reconstruction of Instruction." In *Afro-American Literature: The Reconstruction of Instruction*, 8–24. New York: Modern Language Association, 1979.

Stowe, Harriet Beecher. *A Key to* Uncle Tom's Cabin; *Presenting the Original Facts and Documents upon Which the Story Is Founded together with Corroborative Statements Verifying the Truth of the Work*. 1853. Port Washington, N.Y.: Kennikat, 1968.

Stowe, Harriet Beecher. *Uncle Tom's Cabin*. 1853. New York: Airmont, 1967.

Tate, Claudia. "Allegories of Black Female Desire; or, Rereading Nineteenth-Century Sentimental Narratives of Black Female Authority." In *Changing Our Own Words: Essays on Criticism, Theory, and Writing by Black Women*, ed. Cheryl A. Wall, 98–126. New Brunswick, N.J.: Rutgers University Press, 1989.

Todorov, Tzvetan. *The Fantastic: A Structural Approach to a Literary Genre.* Trans. Richard Howard. Cleveland, Ohio: University of Case Western Reserve Press, 1973.

Todorov, Tzvetan. *The Poetics of Prose.* Trans. Richard Howard. Ithaca, N.Y.: Cornell University Press, 1977.

Tompkins, Jane. *Sensational Designs: The Cultural Work of American Fiction, 1790–1860.* New York: Oxford University Press, 1985.

Ullman, Victor. *Martin R. Delany: The Beginnings of Black Nationalism.* Boston: Beacon, 1971.

Williams, James. *Narrative of James Williams, An American Slave; Who Was for Several Years a Driver on a Cotton Plantation in Alabama.* Dictated to John Greenleaf Whittier. New York: American Anti-Slavery Society, 1838.

Wilson, Harriet E. *Our Nig: or, Sketches from the Life of a Free Black, in a Two-Story House, North, Showing That Slavery's Shadows Fall Even There.* 1859. New York: Vintage, 1983.

Yarborough, Richard. "Race, Violence, and Manhood: The Masculine Ideal in Frederick Douglass's 'The Heroic Slave.'" In *Frederick Douglass: New Literary and Historical Essays*, ed. Eric J. Sundquist, 166–88. Cambridge: Cambridge University Press, 1990.

Yee, Shirley J. *Black Women Abolitionists: A Study in Activism, 1828–1860.* Knoxville: University of Tennessee Press, 1992.

Yellin, Jean Fagin. "Text and Contexts of Harriet Jacobs' *Incidents in the Life of a Slave Girl: Written by Herself.*" In *The Slave's Narrative,* ed. Charles T. Davis and Henry Louis Gates, Jr., 262–82. New York: Oxford University Press, 1985.

Wisconsin Studies in Autobiography

William L. Andrews
General Editor

Robert F. Sayre
*The Examined Self: Benjamin Franklin, Henry Adams,
Henry James*

Daniel B. Shea
Spiritual Autobiography in Early America

Lois Mark Stalvey
The Education of a WASP

Margaret Sams
*Forbidden Family: A Wartime Memoir of the Philippines,
1941–1945*
Edited, with an introduction, by Lynn Z. Bloom

Charlotte Perkins Gilman
*The Living of Charlotte Perkins Gilman: An
Autobiography*
Introduction by Ann J. Lane

Mark Twain
*Mark Twain's Own Autobiography: The Chapters from the
North American Review*
Edited, with an introduction, by Michael Kiskik

*Journeys in New Worlds: Early American Women's
Narratives*
Edited by William L. Andrews

American Autobiography: Retrospect and Prospect
Edited by Paul John Eakin

Caroline Seabury
The Diary of Caroline Seabury, 1854–1863
Edited, with an introduction, by Suzanne L. Bunkers

Marian Anderson
My Lord, What a Morning
Introduction by Nellie Y. McKay

American Women's Autobiography: Fea(s)ts of Memory
Edited, with an introduction, by Margo Culley

Frank Marshall Davis
Livin' the Blues: Memoirs of a Black Journalist and Poet
Edited, with an introduction, by John Edgar Tidwell

Joanne Jacobson
Authority and Alliance in the Letters of Henry Adams

Cornelia Peake McDonald
A Woman's Civil War: A Diary with Reminiscences of the War, from March 1862
Edited, with an introduction, by Minrose C. Gwin

Kamau Brathwaite
The Zea Mexican Diary: 7 Sept. 1926–7 Sept. 1986
Foreword by Sandra Pouchet Paquet

Genaro M. Padilla
My History, Not Yours: The Formation of Mexican American Autobiography